Revise for Geography GCSE AQA Specification B

John Smith

Heinemann Educational Publishers
Halley Court, Jordan Hill, Oxford, OX2 8EJ
Part of Harcourt Education Ltd.

Heinemann is the registered trademark of Harcourt Education Ltd.

Text © John Smith

First published 1998
Second edition 2002

06
10 9 8 7 6 5 4

British Library Cataloguing in Publication Data is available from the British Library on request.

10-digit ISBN 0 435099 93 0
13-digit ISBN 978 0 435099 93 0

Typeset and designed by Magnet Harlequin, Oxford
Revised by AMR Ltd, Sherborne St. John, Hants
Printed and bound in the UK by CPI Bath

Acknowledgements
Every effort has been made to contact copyright holders of material reproduced in this book. Any omissions will be rectified in subsequent printings if notice is given to the publishers.

Contents

Page

How to use this book 4

The United Kingdom 7

1 River basins and their management 7
2 Farming, food and the environment 16
3 Tourism in a glacial environment: the Lake District National Park 25
4 Electricity generation for the future 34
5 The changing location of manufacturing industry 41
6 Understanding the modern urban environment 48

The European Union 61

7 Rich and poor regions in the European Union 61
8 Farming in southern Italy: problems and development in the periphery 63
9 Tourism in Mediterranean Spain 68
10 Development of the European urban core 72
    (a) Rotterdam/Europort 72
    (b) the Ruhr conurbation 77
    (c) the Paris region 83
    (d) the Milan/Turin/Genoa industrial triangle 86
11 The links between eastern England and the EU 91

The wider world 95

12 Amazonia: development in the rainforest environment 95
13 The Ganges delta: dense population in a high-risk environment 102
14 Japan: urbanisation and industrialisation in a resource-poor environment 115

Global issues 122

15 Population growth and urbanisation 122
16 Aid, investment and international development 129
17 Global warming: its causes and consequences 134

Short-answer questions, answers and advice on the exam questions 136

Index 144

How to use this book

One of the great advantages of studying geography is that it is all about real places and real processes. We can see geography going on in the world around us all the time. When we study geography we can go out into the field, or we can look at photographs, videos, satellite images, etc. and actually see what we are studying. We can marvel at wonderful and strange places – but we can also find much that is interesting about more familiar, local, everyday places.

Geographers therefore try to see **patterns** in what they observe. All cities have certain things in common; all climates are linked together by the circulation of the winds; all rivers erode, transport and deposit material; and so on. Geographers have developed a series of key concepts or key ideas or theories to describe these patterns. When they know the key ideas well they can predict many things about new places, because they fit patterns that have already been studied. There are also special features about places, which make each one different from all other places. We have to study the patterns, but also the special features that make places unique and give them their 'sense of place'.

AQA Specification B

Many GCSE specifications provide teachers and students with a set of key ideas, then leave them to choose which areas they study to illustrate those ideas. Specification B starts off by choosing areas that **must** be studied, and then picks out key ideas which can be seen clearly in those chosen regions. There are three scales of study:

- the United Kingdom (UK)
- the European Union (EU)
- the wider world.

In the specification content for the UK, some areas of study have been specified clearly. For example, everyone has to study:

- farming in East Anglia and the Lake District
- ports on the east coast
- high-tech industry in the M4 corridor

and so on. Each of the specified regions is thought to be the best place to study a particular key idea.

However, with some other topics teachers and students are left free to choose exactly which areas they study. The reason for this is that it would be rather unfair for a school in Birmingham to have to study urban growth and change in Manchester, for instance, when the key ideas could be illustrated just as well in their own city.

When people move on to study the EU and the wider world the areas of study are specified very clearly. In the EU you must study:

- the core and the periphery
- farming in southern Italy
- tourism in Mediterranean Spain
- *one* urban area in the European core.

In the wider world you must study Amazonia, the Ganges delta and Japan.

You must remember, though, whether you (or your teacher) have chosen certain places to study, or whether the specification has told you particular areas that you must study. You will be expected to have detailed knowledge of real places to gain high-level marks in the exam. Facts must be learnt!

Each paper in the exam has a quite separate content. Learn the UK topics for Paper 1 and the EU and the wider world topics for Paper 2.

The structure of the assessment

There are three parts to the assessment for AQA Specification B.

Paper 1 consists of questions on the UK. Both the Foundation and Higher tier papers are 1¼ hours long. They consist of four structured questions, and all of them must be answered. At least one question will be based on an Ordnance Survey map at a scale of 1:50 000. This paper is worth 30 per cent of the final mark.

Paper 2 consists of questions on the EU, the wider world and global issues. The global issues are topics of concern throughout the modern world. Each issue is linked back to topics studied in the UK, the EU and/or the wider world. Paper 2 lasts for 2 hours and is worth 45 per cent of the final mark.

The questions on both Paper 1 and Paper 2 are structured. Each paper begins with a section of short-answer questions. Then there are longer, structured questions. The short-answer questions might include multiple choice questions, filling in blanks, one-word or short-phrase answers, etc. Other questions have to be answered in extended writing. Detailed knowledge of case studies is required on both papers.

Coursework consists of a single geographical enquiry. It is worth 25 per cent of the final mark. It is not tiered.

How does this book use case studies?

Case studies form a very important part of all geography courses. They are studies of real places. They illustrate the key ideas that also form part of the course. For example, when you are studying glaciated landscapes, you look at:

- general ideas about how ice erodes

- general ideas about the formation of physical features like corries, arêtes and U-shaped valleys

- examples of these features and the way they fit together to form a landscape – for example, you could study the Helvellyn region of the Lake District as a case study to show how the processes have formed a real place.

In your exam you will be asked to 'refer to examples you have studied' or to 'illustrate your answer with references to case studies'. When you answer these questions you **must** write about real places. The examiner will check to see whether you write with a **sense of place**. In other words, you need to show that you know why a particular place is special, or different from other places. You need to know names and details of features in the area that you are describing. If you include plenty of precise detail, the answer becomes a good one and your mark gets better.

Some revision books give detailed case studies for the whole Geography GCSE course. This book gives detailed studies for areas that are specified in the specification, especially places in the EU and the wider world. However, some parts of the specification, mostly in the UK section, do not specify which places should be studied. Key ideas are given which can be illustrated by any case study, and any good example can be used.

You have spent two years studying a set of case studies. If this book gave you a completely new set you could waste a lot of time. Learning new case studies at this stage of the course could mean a lot of extra work, and may create a lot of confusion too. So this book tries to help you to *use the examples from your class work in the most efficient way possible*.

When you have to refer to one of your own case studies there is a box in the text headed 'Case Study questions'. This suggests what is essential to learn from any relevant place you have studied. At this point you could:

- write notes in your notebook (or in this book, if it is your own)

- write a summary of your case study in your notebook or clip it into this book

- write down page references in your notebook or in this book, to show which page of your exercise or textbook contains the information needed.

Marginal notes

Special notes are included on the right-hand side of many pages. These are simply some facts and ideas that could be used in your exam answers. Try to remember them, though they are not always key ideas.

Hints and Tips! These give general advice and useful information about how to prepare for and then sit the examination. Following this advice could stop you wasting time and effort *and* help you improve your grade.

 These are useful facts and ideas that could provide helpful points in some of your exam answers.

This is useful additional information about certain points in the text.

Focus Point One piece of advice for preparing for exams is: '**Active revision** (or doing things to help you remember) is usually better than **passive revision** (or just reading)'. The Focus Points give you little tasks to do to check that you are remembering what you have read.

Do the tasks set. Jot down your answers in your notebook, or ask a friend or parent to test you. Be honest with yourself.

- If you do well you should be pleased.

- If you do badly, do not despair. Just re-read the section, but more carefully this time. Then test yourself again and hope to do better.

- You have tested your 'short-term memory'. How long will the information stick? Next time you come to do some revision you may well test yourself again. Renewing your revision like this often helps transfer the information into your medium or long-term memory, which is very important for the exam.

- Many of the Focus Points ask you for four or five facts. Often two or three will be enough in the exam. So, why learn five?
  – It gives you something in reserve.
  – All the facts may not go into your long-term memory – but some will.
  – A full list of points helps you to *understand* as well as to learn.

Test questions

Most sections end with a test question, similar to the ones you may face in the exam. After each part of these questions there is a note like this: **(3 marks)**

This tells you how many marks the question is worth. It also provides a rough guide to the amount of detail needed in your answer.

- A 1 mark question usually requires a single word or short sentence.

- 2 mark questions may need two simple points, or they may need one point that has been elaborated or developed. Often the Hints and Tips (see above) explain how to develop and elaborate your answers.

- 3 mark questions almost certainly need some development of ideas – but usually only require three or four lines of writing. If you write much more you may be wasting time. If you write much less your answer may lack detail.

- When more marks are available the answer usually needs extended writing. Here are real chances to show your detailed knowledge and understanding. These longer answers usually need careful reference to your case studies.

Pages 136–143 give mark schemes, specimen answers and some advice on the best way to answer the questions.

Finally . . .

Good luck. Work hard, but . . .

- Try to enjoy your revision. It should be very satisfying to see the whole subject come together at the end of the course. You become a real geographer in this way, and real geographers impress examiners!

- Don't panic. Methodical, careful, steady work is far better than desperate over-cramming.

- Fit, relaxed, alert people do better in exams than burnt-out swotaholics.

- In the last few weeks before the exam, practise topics that you are not so good at. Do not just concentrate on what you are comfortable with. Work hard on your areas of weakness.

The United Kingdom

1 River basins and their management

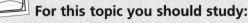

For this topic you should study:
- the hydrological cycle
- processes of erosion (hydraulic processes, attrition, abrasion and solution), transportation (suspension, saltation, traction and in solution) and deposition
- landforms in uplands (V-shaped valleys, interlocking spurs, waterfalls) and lowlands (flood plains, meanders, ox-bow lakes)
- watershed, drainage basin, catchment area
- water supplies from a reservoir, and from an area of groundwater supplies
- water management – flood control, pollution control, leisure and environment.

The hydrological cycle (or water cycle) shows how water is transferred from the sea to the land, then back again to the sea. Diagrams showing the cycle are very simplified. They often show all the water that falls onto the land flowing back to the sea, over the surface, as run-off. The full picture is more complicated, as a study of drainage basins shows.

Still, it is important to understand the basic features of the hydrological cycle. These show energy from the sun evaporating water. This evaporation can happen over land as well as over the sea.

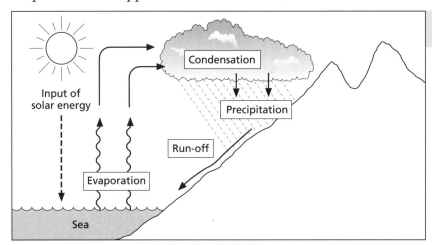

◀ Figure 1.1
The hydrological cycle

 **ocus Point 1**

Cover the page and draw a labelled diagram showing evaporation, condensation, precipitation and run-off in the water cycle.

Learn this precisely.

Water vapour is then carried over the land, by winds. Here the air may be cooled, causing condensation, followed by precipitation.

The movement of water through a drainage basin

Water is input into the drainage basin by **precipitation**. This can take the form of rain, snow, sleet, hail, dew or frost. Then the water can pass through several types of **transfer**, or be kept in several different **stores**.

Transfers	Stores
Unchannelled surface flow	Snowfields or ice caps
Channelled flow in rivers	Lakes, ponds, puddles, etc.
Soil throughflow	Soil moisture storage
Groundwater flow	Groundwater storage (in permeable rocks)
Take-up by plants	
Evaporation*/Evapo-transpiration*	Storage as plant moisture

* These two transfers take water out of the river system.

Note: The transfers and stores listed are all natural processes. People can store water in reservoirs, tanks, etc. They can even pump water into the rocks to top up groundwater supplies for future use. Then they can transfer water along pipes, canals, etc. They can also pump water into rivers so that water supplies are transferred through these cheap, natural systems.

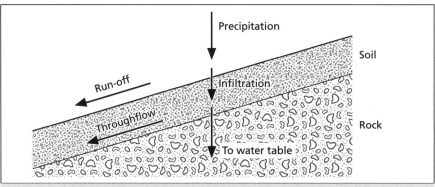

▲ *Figure 1.2 What happens to precipitation when it reaches the surface?*

Exactly which route water takes through the river system depends on many interrelated factors. These include:

Intensity of the rainfall – during light rain much of the water soaks into the ground. When rain is heavier it cannot all infiltrate. Run-off increases.

Length of rainfall period – if there has been a long period of rainfall the ground may be saturated. If there is any more rain it will lead to surface run-off.

Nature of the rock – if the rock is permeable (e.g. limestone) water can soak into it, and be stored as groundwater. Impermeable rock (such as shale) will not let water soak in, and this also increases run-off.

Vegetation cover – plant leaves intercept rainfall. This can slow it down, meaning it does not run off as quickly. Plant roots help to break up the soil, and allow water to infiltrate more easily, also reducing run-off.

Building and farming – when the surface is built over, with houses or tarmac, water cannot infiltrate. This increases the rate of run-off. Overgrazing by animals can compact the soil, and make infiltration difficult. The weight of heavy machinery on the land can also do this.

In fact, anything that reduces infiltration, or reduces the amount of water stored in the soil, or increases the rate of run-off, helps cause flooding. This is because these all lead to more water reaching the river quickly. When it all arrives at the same time, floods may result.

All rain is caused when air rises and cools, leading to condensation. The air can be forced to rise in three different ways: by convection, by relief, or at a front.

ocus Point 2

Cover the page, then list parts of the hydrological cycle: three natural transfers, three natural stores, two human transfers, and two human stores.

Remember: the faster rainwater gets to the stream, the more likely it is to cause a flood.

What is a drainage basin?

A river is a channel of running water. It is fed by water that runs into it, from a wide area. Some water reaches the main river through smaller rivers or **tributaries**. These join the main stream at **confluences**.

Any water that falls onto the surface in between the river and its tributaries runs towards one of the streams. It may flow over the surface (as **run-off**) or through the soil (as **throughflow**). At the bottom of slopes there is usually a stream, flowing in a **valley**.

The whole area drained by a main river and its tributaries is called a **drainage basin**. A basin is usually surrounded by higher land – except at the coast, where the river joins the sea. The highest land, which separates one river basin from the next, is called the **watershed**.

The map on page 102 shows the drainage basin of the Ganges river. To the north are the Himalayas and to the south is the Deccan Plateau. The river flows into the Bay of Bengal, through its **delta**. Here the river splits up into a number of smaller channels, called **distributaries**.

Landforms in drainage basins

As water moves through the drainage basin it has energy. Some of the energy is used to do 'work' of **erosion** and **transportation** of rock and soil. If the energy available to the river is reduced it cannot do so much work, so some of the material that was being transported is **deposited**.

Focus Point 3

Would these actions make a flood more likely or less likely?
(a) Cutting down an area of woodland and ploughing the soil.
(b) Putting drains into an area of marshland, so that it can be used for arable crops.
(c) Reducing the size of a flock of sheep, to stop them over-grazing the land.
(d) Building a new housing estate on a hillside in a drainage basin.

The amount of energy available is greatest when:	The amount of energy decreases when:
• the river is flowing steeply downhill	• the river's course becomes gentler
• the river contains a large volume of water.	• the volume of water in the river decreases.

Rivers erode by:

- **Hydraulic action** where the power of the moving water simply forces particles of rock away from the bed.
- **Abrasion** when the river knocks and rubs the material it is carrying against the bed, and this breaks more particles off the bed.
- **Attrition** where particles of rock being transported are rubbed together, and against the bed, and are worn away by the friction.
- **Solution** where rock is dissolved as the river flows over it.

Four forms of transportation can also be seen. They are shown on the diagram below.

Hints and Tips!

Learn the headings (here, for erosion) first. Once you have learnt them it gives you a structure to fit the details into. This makes the details easier to learn.

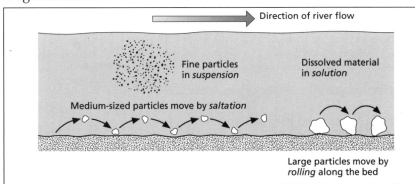

◄ *Figure 1.3 Movement of particles transported by a river*

Landforms in the upper sections

In the upland sections most of a river's spare energy is used to erode its bed. The bed is lowered more quickly than material can be removed from the sides. This produces a steep, V-shaped valley cross-section. As the river gets closer to sea-level the rate of downcutting gets slower and the sides are eroded more quickly. This means that the valley broadens out to form more gently sloping sides.

ocus Point 4

Cover the previous page, then list the four ways that a river erodes, and the four ways that a river transports material.

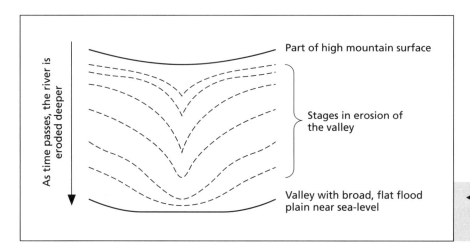

As time passes, the river is eroded deeper

Part of high mountain surface

Stages in erosion of the valley

Valley with broad, flat flood plain near sea-level

◄ *Figure 1.4 Stages in the erosion of a river valley*

Rivers never flow straight for a long distance. They always bend or meander. This produces the interlocking spurs that are found in river valleys in highland areas. As the rivers cuts its valley deeper into the rock the bends are cut into the surface. This leaves the area of land on the inside of each bend as a ridge of high land. The river twists and turns between these ridges, which are known as **interlocking spurs**.

DID YOU KNOW ?

Some people think that interlocking spurs look like the teeth of a giant-sized zip.

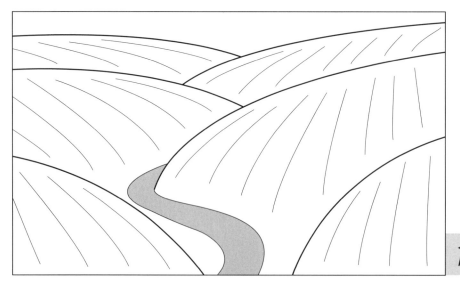

◄ *Figure 1.5 Interlocking spurs*

Sometimes a river bed is formed of a layer of hard rock which cannot easily be eroded. When the river passes from the hard rock onto softer rock it is suddenly able to erode its bed easily, and so there is a sudden fall in the bed. This produces a **waterfall**.

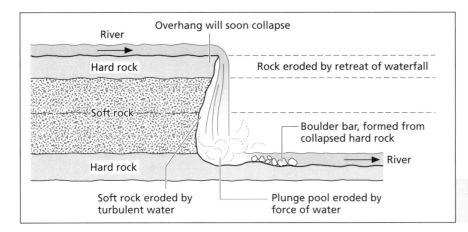

◀ *Figure 1.6 Formation of a waterfall*

Often a deep, steep-sided gorge forms downstream from a waterfall. This is because the water going over the falls has a sudden increase of energy. This can be used to undercut the hard rock at the top of the waterfall. The waterfall gradually retreats up the stream, leaving the gorge between the remains of the layer of hard rock.

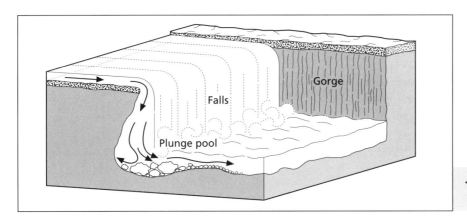

◀ *Figure 1.7 A gorge below a waterfall*

Landforms in the lower section

The diagram 'Stages in erosion of a river valley' on the previous page shows how V-shaped upland streams broaden out as they approach sea-level. Near the sea rivers flow in wide, flat valleys which cannot be eroded downwards, because they are so near sea-level. The rivers are broad and deep, so there is little friction with the sides. The rivers have plenty of energy, so they can transport a lot of sediment.

However, when a river floods it spreads out over a wider area. There is far more friction with the wider bed. Less energy is available for transportation, so a lot of sediment is suddenly dropped by the river. The whole flood plain can be covered with a thin layer of fine sediment. If this is repeated many times, a deep layer of rich soil can be built up on the flood plain.

Deposition on flood plains can be seen in parts of the UK but it is even more obvious in river valleys like the Ganges and Brahmaputra in India and Bangladesh. See chapter 13.

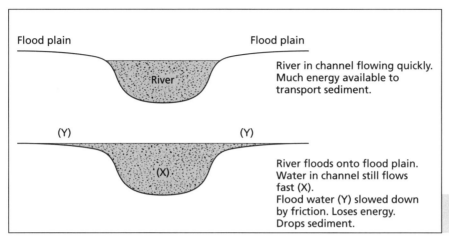

River in channel flowing quickly. Much energy available to transport sediment.

River floods onto flood plain. Water in channel still flows fast (X).
Flood water (Y) slowed down by friction. Loses energy. Drops sediment.

◀ *Figure 1.8 Flood plain formation*

As rivers flow across their flood plains they meander. The main current swings from side to side as it flows, and this leads to erosion being concentrated first on one bank then on the other. Deposition always takes place on the opposite bank. Meanders form, and then grow. This can lead to the formation of ox-bow lakes.

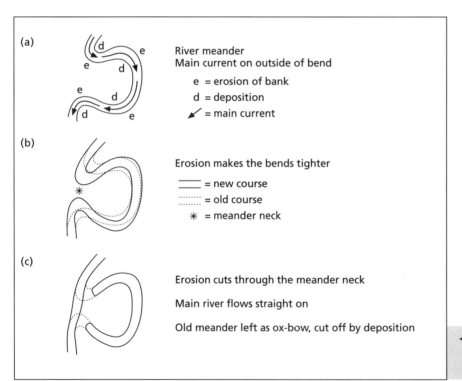

(a) River meander
Main current on outside of bend

   e = erosion of bank
   d = deposition
   ✎ = main current

(b) Erosion makes the bends tighter

   ——— = new course
   ········· = old course
   ＊ = meander neck

(c) Erosion cuts through the meander neck

Main river flows straight on

Old meander left as ox-bow, cut off by deposition

Hints and Tips!

You need to know examples of all the above features located in the UK.

◀ *Figure 1.9 Meanders and ox-bow lake formation*

Management of water in drainage basins

Water supply

The two maps below show that some of the heaviest rainfall totals in the UK are in areas with sparse population. Some of the areas of dense population have only moderate rainfall.

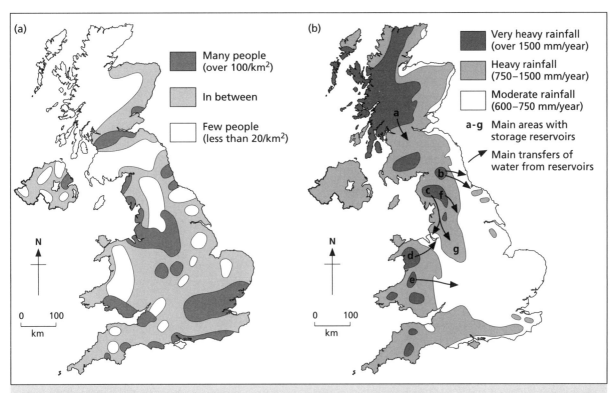

▲ *Figure 1.10 Population density, rainfall and water supply in the UK*
(a) Population density   (b) Rainfall and water supply

One of the main aims of water management is to store water which falls in places and at times when it is not needed; and to transfer it to the places where it is needed. These maps show how reservoirs are used for storage in wet, sparsely populated highlands. Then the water is transferred to the drier, densely populated lowland areas for industry, agriculture and domestic use.

 **ocus Point 5**

Study the two maps above (Figure 1.10) along with a relief map of Britain in an atlas. Learn the names of the highland regions where precipitation totals are highest.

Questions

1 Choose an example of a reservoir in highland Britain.
   • Why was the reservoir built there?
   • What area does it serve?

2 Think about any of the issues involved in the construction of the reservoir and its system of water transfer.
   Can the reservoir be used for other purposes, such as leisure?

In other areas water is obtained from boreholes, from rivers, or by treating and recycling waste water. Figure 1.11 shows how these three sources of water are used to supply Greater London.

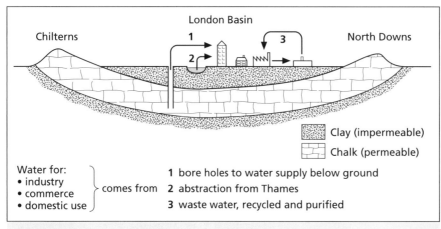

▲ *Figure 1.11 Greater London's water sources*

Flood control

Water authorities are responsible for trying to reduce the flood hazard caused by rivers. Some of the causes of floods are described at the beginning of this chapter. Ways of controlling floodwater include:

Reafforestation schemes – to increase evapotranspiration, reduce run-off and to hold the soil together.

Advising on land use – to try to reduce over-stocking and other farming practices that increase flood risk.

Clearing and straightening streams – to remove obstructions and speed flow of water through the system.

Zoning land use on flood plains – There are strict regulations to stop building in areas with a serious flood risk, and to allow only non-residential building in areas with some flood risk.

Controlling river pollution

The water authorities and the Environment Agency share responsibility for controlling river pollution. In 1990 over 60 per cent of rivers in England and Wales were described as being of 'good quality', with another 25 per cent described as 'fair quality'. However, 11 per cent were 'poor' or 'bad'. In 1991 there were almost 30 000 reported pollution incidents. The table shows where these came from.

The authorities first trace the source of the pollution then get it stopped. They try to prevent further incidents by talking to polluters. They may take them to court if negotiation and persuasion fail.

Untreated sewage	28%
Oil spills and leaks	24%
Farm spills and leaks*	13%
Industrial waste	12%
Other sources†	23%

* As well as reported incidents there is regular infiltration of chemicals from fertilisers etc. spread on the land.

† Including pollution from roads, power stations, landfill sites, leisure activities, etc.

Managing water for leisure

The leisure industry is the fastest-growing area of employment in the world. It is very important in the UK. Many people spend a large part of their leisure on or next to water, boating, fishing, swimming, canoeing, bird watching, surfboarding, and doing many more such pastimes.

Many rivers and reservoirs are used for **multipurpose schemes**. Water that is being stored for water supply or HEP is also used for leisure pursuits. This multiple use of water needs very careful management.

- Is the water that is needed for leisure clean?
- Can the authorities be sure that leisure use does not pollute drinking water?
- Can conflict between the different users be reduced or stopped?
- Should leisure users be asked to pay for using the water?

Focus Point 6

List three ways in which planting forests helps to reduce flooding.

List three other ways in which people plan to reduce the problems caused by flooding in river basins.

Questions

Refer to a reservoir or river that has multiple uses.

1 Describe the varied uses.
2 Explain how potential conflicts between users are managed and resolved.

Exam practice

(a) Choose **one** of the features of a river valley listed below:

- waterfall   • ox-bow lake.

(i) Name a place where an example of this feature can be found. (1 mark)
(ii) Describe the appearance of your named feature. (3 marks)
(iii) Using one or more diagrams, explain how the feature was formed. (5 marks)

(b) (i) Explain why London is able to get a large part of its water supply from rocks below the city. (3 marks)
(ii) Name two other major sources of water for the people of London. (2 marks)

(c) (i) Name a highland area which is used to supply water for a major city. (1 mark)
(ii) Name the city that the water is supplied to. (1 mark)
(iii) Describe some of the other activities that often take place on and around water storage reservoirs. (4 marks)

2 Farming, food and the environment

For this topic you should study:
- inputs, processes and outputs of a commercial farm
- the influences of the natural environment on farming systems in the UK.

You should make particular studies of:
- hill sheep farming in the Lake District: a farm case study with reference to
  - physical constraints of landform, climate and soil, including a study of relief rainfall
  - the influence of CAP subsidies, government policy and competition in the global market leading to diversification
- arable farming in East Anglia: a farm case study with reference to
  - the physical advantages of landform, climate and soil
  - the influence of CAP subsidies, government policy and competition in the global market
  - the demands of supermarket chains and food processing firms
  - the environmental impact of high-input farming on habitats, and attempts to reduce these impacts.

Classification of farms

The natural environment – soil, climate, slope and relief – has a big effect on what can be grown on any farm. It allows some crops to be grown, but makes it impossible to grow certain others. For instance, in East Anglia wheat, grass, barley, rye, oats and sugar beet will all grow, but rice and bananas will not, because the temperature is too low. In other words, the farmer can choose what to grow, within limits.

The human environment also affects the farmer's decisions. What he chooses depends on his knowledge, skills and interests and also on the prices he can get for each crop at the market. He is also influenced by government policies which may make some crops more attractive by paying subsidies, and may make others less attractive by putting quotas (or limits) on the amount that can be grown.

It is very useful for geographers to be able to classify farms into different groups. It makes studying farming easier if we identify the key features of different farming systems. All farms – in the UK and in other parts of the world – can be classified in three ways. These put farms in groups depending on their inputs, processes and outputs.

Note Some geographers think that human influences on farmers are more important than physical influences these days. Farmers can change the physical environment using technology – but they cannot change the needs of the market. The policies of the European Union also have an enormous effect on what farmers produce.

Hints and Tips!

You should try to learn the three classifications that follow.

First learn the shapes of the tables and the headings in each box. This gives you a structure, so later it is much easier to learn the detail under each heading.

Classification by inputs

INTENSIVE FARMING	EXTENSIVE FARMING
These farms have large amounts of inputs on a comparatively small area of land. They are usually found on good land. Money and time invested in such land will bring good profits for the farmer. **Capital intensive** Invests a lot of money in machinery, seeds, fertilisers, irrigation, etc. **Labour intensive** Puts a lot of work into a small area of land. **Capital and labour intensive** Invests a lot of money, and uses a lot of labour.	These farms have comparatively small inputs for large areas of land. They are usually found where conditions are poor, so it is not worth farmers putting a lot of money or work into the land.

Classification by processes

Arable	Pastoral
Grows crops, mainly cereals such as wheat, barley, maize and sugar beet.	Keeps animals for meat, milk, wool, etc.
Mixed Usually combines arable farming with keeping some animals.	**Market gardening** Grows fruit, flowers or vegetables.

Note Mixed farming used to be **very** common in most parts of England. In the last 40 years farming has gradually become more specialised, often because of pressure from the government or the EU. This means that mixed farms are now less common here.

Classification by outputs

Commercial	Subsistence
The outputs from the farm are mainly or entirely for sale.	The outputs of the farm are eaten or used by the family who run the farm. In good years there may be some produce left over for sale.
Mainly subsistence	
The family rely on food produced on the farm, but always plan to try and produce some surplus for sale.	

Farm systems

ocus Point 1

Cover the page then write simple definitions of:

- arable
- pastoral
- subsistence
- commercial
- labour intensive
- capital intensive
- extensive.

Hints and Tips!

Two farm case studies are summarised over the page. More detail about these farms can be found in *GCSE Geography for AQA Specification B* by Helm and Robinson. You should learn the key facts from the summaries in as much detail as possible.

Lake District: Waterside House Farm

Physical inputs
Temperature
- summer 15°C in valley, lower on fells
- winter 5°C in valley, lower on fells

Rainfall 1476mm/year in valley, higher on fells
Soil
- in valley – some silty, so heavy; some gravely, so well-drained
- on fells – thin and stony, with acid peat on high, flat land

Slopes gentle near lake, with steep, glaciated valley sides rising to rugged fell

Human inputs
Labour
- farmer and son plus one casual worker at busy times
- full-time worker on campsite in summer

Capital inputs
Machinery tractor, baler for silage
Chemical inputs sheep dip to kill parasites, limited fertiliser on silage meadows, spray to kill bracken

THE FARM
Area of land 113ha plus grazing rights to fell – 69ha
Buildings tractor shed, silage store, sheds for lambing of weak ewes
Animals 880 ewes produce 950 lambs

Main processes
- sheep winter on inbye and intake land; lamb near farm
- in May, move onto intake land and fell; silage made in early summer
- shearing; sales; dipping; mating

Outputs
- wool to merchant in Bradford for carpets
- 475 fat lambs for slaughter and export to Europe
- 325 female lambs sold to other farms for breeding
- (150 lambs kept for breeding)

Other sources of income
- EU guarantee prices of lambs, but only up to the quota of 880 sheep
- CAP subsidy for 'severely disadvantaged status' – harsh environment
- ESA payments (Environmentally Sensitive Area) to maintain and increase habitat diversity
- Campsite on edge of lake for 120 tents from March to October
- Canoes and boats for hire on Ullswater

East Anglia: Lynford House Farm

Physical inputs
Temperature
- summer 16°C
- winter 16°C

Rainfall 559mm/year
Sunshine high totals
Soil alluvium and peat – very fertile
Slopes flat, just above sea level, much drained marshland

Human inputs
Labour 5 full time workers plus contract workers employed for harvesting

Capital inputs
Machinery several tractors, combine harvesters, sprays, fertiliser spreaders, ventilated potato store, etc.
Chemical inputs large amounts of fertilisers, pesticides, insecticides – bought through a co-operative
Other input 55 000 cubic metre reservoir for irrigation water

THE FARM
Area of land 570ha
Buildings machinery sheds, storage buildings
Animals none

Main processes
- wheat: plough (Aug), sow (Sept), fertilise, spray, harvest (Jul)
- potatoes: plough (Nov – Jan), fertilise, plant (Apr), spray, irrigate, harvest (Oct)
- sugar beet: fertilise (Nov), plough (Dec – Feb), sow (Mar), spray, harvest (Oct)
- peas: plough (Nov, Mar), sow (Apr), spray, harvest (Jul)

Outputs
- 3000 tonnes of potatoes to supermarket chain
- 400 tonnes of peas to canning company
- sugar beet to factory at Ely (10 km)
- wheat to grain merchant plus surplus unsold goes into EU storage

Other sources of income
- EU intervention price paid for wheat that cannot be sold
- 55 ha (hectares) of land in set-aside – EU pays to leave land out of production
- 10 out of 12 workers' bungalows on the farm are being sold or hired to non-farm workers
- small wind farm, pays £3000 per year per turbine

Relief rainfall and farming in the UK

One of the main differences between the environments of the Lake District and East Anglia is in terms of their rainfall.

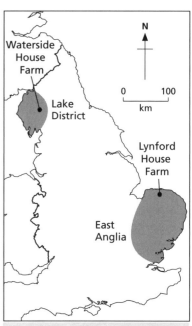

▲ Figure 2.1 The Lake District and East Anglia

	Rainfall in the Lake District	Rainfall in East Anglia
Total	At least 1000 mm/year.	Below 750 mm/year everywhere.
	Over 2000 mm/year in places.	Below 600 mm/year in places.
Distribution	All year round but autumn/winter maximum.	All year round but late summer maximum.
Cause	Relief and frontal rainfall.	Frontal, with convective rainfall in summer.

The diagram below shows why the Lake District receives so much rainfall, and why rainfall totals are much lower in East Anglia.

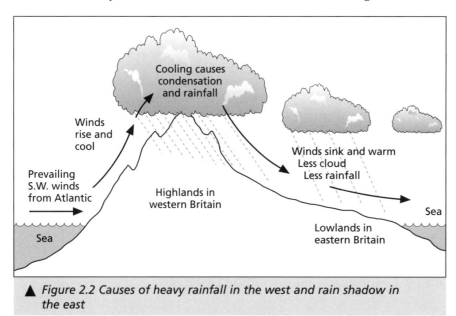

▲ Figure 2.2 Causes of heavy rainfall in the west and rain shadow in the east

Intensive farming and the environment

Until the 1970s almost all farms in the UK were mixed farms. They grew some crops and kept some animals. This had a number of advantages:

- Animals provided manure to help fertilise the soil.

- Crops were fed to animals, and meat made more profit than cereals.

- The workload was spread out through the year.

- If the weather was bad for one product, something else did well.

- Different crops used different minerals from the soil. Rotation kept the soil fertile.

However, from the 1970s arable farmers began to specialise in just one or two crops. This was mainly because **subsidies** were paid by the EU. It was also a result of the need to buy specialised machinery, and to develop specialised skills in the workforce. Mechanisation and the development of **monoculture** (production of a single crop) did cause problems, but farmers came up with solutions to these. Unfortunately the solutions often caused new problems.

Problem	Solution	New problems
No animals on farms = no manure, so less fertile soil.	Increase the input of chemical fertilisers.	Overuse of chemicals pollutes soil, rivers and drinking water.
Monoculture = less crop rotation so nutrients not replaced.	Increase the input of chemical fertilisers.	Loss of wildlife, because of chemicals and loss of habitat.
Monoculture = large areas with one crop so disease spreads easily.	Increase the input of pesticides.	
Mechanisation = more space needed for machines to work efficiently.	Pull up hedgerows to make fewer, larger fields. Drain wetlands.	Soil erosion. Loss of beauty in the landscape.
Overproduction = too much crop grown so price falls.	EU guarantees prices and stores surpluses.	High cost to taxpayers.

Diversification of farming

In the last few decades farmers intensified production; now they are being encouraged to cut production in some areas. **Diversification** means that farmers are encouraged to look for new ways of using the land. In some areas of the country farmers can receive subsidies for some or all of the following developments:

- farming land by less intensive, traditional methods to encourage wild flowers to grow in grassland

- replanting hedgerows, and trimming them in such a way that they provide good habitats for a variety of wild animals and birds

- planting woodland instead of crops

- leaving some areas as wildlife reserves, rather than growing crops

- leaving wetland in its natural state and not draining it, and so on.

Even when there is no new land use, farmers can leave land unused and receive a payment in compensation. This is called **set-aside**, and up to 10 per cent of a farmer's land can be left, or 'set aside'. The aim is to cut overproduction and surpluses kept in storage by the EU. It also gives land

Hints and Tips!

When you know the general ideas shown on this table, you need to learn extra details about the problems by referring to your case study notes. The relevant section in your notes might be headed: 'Intensive farming', 'Drainage of wetlands' or 'Hedgerow removal'.

a chance to lie fallow (rest), and improve its fertility without adding more chemicals. While it is unused it becomes a better habitat for wildlife.

Farmers are also encouraged to diversify their income by using their land for other purposes. For example they may:

- convert old farm buildings as holiday homes
- offer bed and breakfast at the farm
- stock streams with fish and let fishermen pay for the right to fish
- keep unusual animals for meat, such as deer or even ostriches
- use some fields for sports meetings, such as motorbike scrambling.

Chemical inputs and farming in East Anglia

Chemicals are very important for most modern arable farmers. The chemicals that farmers use fall into three main groups:
Fertilisers that add nutrients to the soil to replace those that crops take out. They can be used with, or even instead of, manure.
Insecticides and pesticides that kill insects which might eat crops or damage them in other ways, and pests, such as fungus, which can damage crops during growth or after harvest.
Herbicides that kill weeds which might compete with the crops for nutrients and sunlight.

Without the use of chemicals:

- farmers would not have been able to grow so much of our food
- food prices would have been more expensive
- the food sold in our shops would not look as good and would not be free from blemishes.

However, some people think that too many chemicals have been used and this has led to:

- pollution of water supplies, when excess chemicals have been washed off the land into rivers and down to the water table
- loss of bio-diversity – e.g. killing insects has removed a vital link from the food chain and this has led to loss of birds and mammals from the countryside
- chemical residues on foods which can damage health.

Some farmers still feel that their main aim is to grow plenty of cheap food. The government and the European Union's CAP have encouraged them to do this and so they continue to use high inputs and to produce high outputs. Mr Sears on Lyndford House Farm is a high-input farmer.

Others have become 'organic'. They have decided to reduce their artificial inputs (although they are still allowed to use a very limited range of chemicals). They rely on weeding by hand and by hoeing

Hints and Tips!
This is an ideal topic to show your understanding of how values and attitudes can affect the way different groups see the countryside.

ocus Point 3

Cover up the page then list:

◆ three ways that some farmers can get subsidies for farming to conserve the environment

◆ three ways that farmers can diversify into new ways of using the land.

• Increased use of fertilisers reduced use of manure.	• Less humus returned to soil, so crumb structure was damaged.
• Increased mechanisation.	• Heavy machinery compressed soil, less infiltration of rain water, more run-off.
• Reduction of pastoral farming, grass ploughed up for crops.	• Ploughing leaves soil without vegetation cover, so no roots to protect soil.
• Removal of hedges.	• Nothing to break the force of the wind, so erosion is increased.

▲ *Figure 2.3 How intensive farming can lead to soil erosion*

instead of using herbicides; they use natural manure and compost instead of chemical fertilisers; and they keep a natural balance and rely on birds and other natural predators to keep insects under control.

However, organic production is labour intensive and farmers can only make a profit if they can charge higher prices for their produce. This is called 'the organic premium'. More and more shoppers are willing to pay this premium because they feel that the food is better and because it helps conserve the countryside.

Other farmers follow a middle way. They have reduced the intensity of their farming because they are being paid to plant trees (Farm Woodland Premium Scheme) or replant hedgerows (Countryside Stewardship Scheme). These payments make up for their loss of profits because of reduced production.

Others use 'precision farming'. These farmers obtain data about their fields from satellite images. These images can tell the farmers how well their crops are growing in different parts of each field. They can also provide information about pests and weeds in the fields. When the farmer comes to harvest a field, sensors on the combine harvester record figures for the yields from different parts of the field. Global Positioning Systems (GPS) and computers in the tractor cab use this data to produce very accurate yield maps.

Then, using all this data, farmers can plan *exactly* where fertiliser is needed. None is wasted on parts of the field which have low yields. The data about pests and weeds tells the farmer *exactly* where and when he needs to spray. If he sprays early enough he can often stop an infestation before it spreads. So he can reduce his input of pesticide or herbicide but make sure it goes exactly where it is needed.

Precision farming means that the farmer can reduce inputs but target them more efficiently. He cuts his costs but does not reduce output. This is a real win-win situation. It shows how technology can be used to help the farmer, the consumer and the environment.

Hints and Tips!

The CAP is a complex subject, but if you can learn some of the basic ideas included here you could earn marks in the exam.

ocus Point 4

◆ List four changes to farming in East Anglia that have helped to increase soil erosion.

◆ List four ways that farmers have been encouraged to reduce the problem of soil erosion.

Exam practice

(a) (i) The Lake District has heavy rainfall, over 1000mm per year in many places. Draw a labelled diagram to explain how the area's high land helps to cause the heavy rainfall. (5 marks)

    (ii) Explain why East Anglia has average rainfall totals that are lower than those for the Lake District. (4 marks)

(b) Explain why the relief of East Anglia is well suited to arable farming, and why the relief of the Lake District is unsuited to arable farming. (5 marks)

(c) Diversification of land use has become common in many farming areas of the UK. Choose an example of diversification that you have studied in **either** the Lake District **or** East Anglia.

    (i) Describe how diversification of land use has happened.

    (ii) Explain the advantages to the farmer. (6 marks)

Farming and the environment – a last word

Alfie Sutton is a farmer in Long Sleddale on the eastern edge of the Lake District. He says: 'I love this valley, the peace and quiet and the scenery. I know the land, the weather, the vegetation, the stream and the wildlife far better than you visitors ever will. But beautiful views don't put food on my table and diesel in my Land Rover ... so what will happen in the future?

If I stop farming here this area will be ruined. The paths will get overgrown, the walls will fall down, the valley floor will return to marshland, scrub vegetation will replace the green fields with their flowers. The views will be ruined for tourists. So the question is: will the governments of the UK and European Union pay us to become custodians of the landscape? Farming will never be profitable here without subsidies – but the landscape needs to be farmed to keep it attractive to all you visitors. Farmers must be helped to survive.'

3 Tourism in a glacial environment: the Lake District National Park

> **For this topic you should study:**
> - the Lake District National Park, with reference to:
>   - the aims of the National Parks
>   - the characteristics and major landform features of the Lake District, especially upland glaciation
>   - the impact of tourism on the area
>   - pressures such as erosion, conservation, conflicts of land use, and traffic
>   - 'honeypot' sites (issues and possible solutions)

Leisure and tourism is one of the world's most rapidly growing industries. People in more economically developed countries have gained more leisure time and have more money to spend on leisure activities. This means that they are willing to pay people to provide services for them to enjoy in a variety of ways.

Leisure services become concentrated in particular areas – often in areas with specially attractive environments. In this specification, two particular environments are chosen for study. You must study coastal resorts in Mediterranean Spain, and these are covered in chapter 9. The other environment in the UK is the National Parks, especially the Lake District.

Remember, jobs in tourism are usually only seasonal. They cannot be relied on to offer a wage all year round.

The National Parks

There are eleven National Parks in England and Wales although two more are about to be designated. The first National Parks in Britain were set up soon after the Second World War. They had two main aims:

To conserve areas of beautiful and remote countryside.	To encourage people to use these areas for leisure.

It should be clear that, right from the start, there was a potential conflict between these two aims, because:

One of the best ways to conserve the land, is to stop large numbers of people from using it.	If large numbers of people are encouraged to use the land they will almost certainly bring changes.

Another problem arose right from the start. The National Park Authorities do not own the land in the Parks. They just have responsibility for helping to plan how the land is used. In fact most of

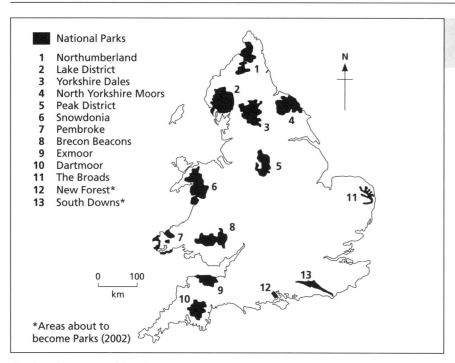

Key:

■ National Parks

1 Northumberland
2 Lake District
3 Yorkshire Dales
4 North Yorkshire Moors
5 Peak District
6 Snowdonia
7 Pembroke
8 Brecon Beacons
9 Exmoor
10 Dartmoor
11 The Broads
12 New Forest*
13 South Downs*

0   100
km

*Areas about to
become Parks (2002)

Figure 3.1 National Parks in England and Wales

ocus Point 1

Cover up the map. Try naming all 13 National Parks. When you can name them all, try to mark them on a blank map of the UK.

ocus Point 2

Cover up the page. What are the two main aims of the National Parks?

What is the 'compromise' aim, which describes what the Park planners actually try to do?

the land is owned by farmers. Large areas are also owned by forestry companies, water boards, the National Trust, the Ministry of Defence, quarrying companies, private householders, etc. There could very easily be conflict between the needs of the land owners and the needs of people wanting to use the land for leisure. So the Park Authorities developed a new aim:

> To try to plan the use of the land so that the needs of all the potential users were met, and so that conflict between the different users was reduced as much as possible.

The Lake District National Park Authority has tried to do this by:

- setting up visitor information and education centres like the National Park Centre at Brockholes on the edge of Windermere

- introducing regulations to control some leisure activities, allowing them in certain areas and stopping them in others (e.g. allowing power boats on parts of Lake Windermere and Coniston, but banning them on other lakes, such as Wastwater)

- improving and maintaining footpaths, so that erosion caused by walkers does not get out of control

- signposting footpaths to help walkers, and to stop them wandering, getting lost, and damaging crops, walls and livestock

- controlling new building and alterations to existing buildings, by introducing strict rules about the type of materials and styles that can be used, and where building can take place.

You cannot understand the nature of tourism in the Lake District without studying the physical background to the area. This involves the study of glaciation and its effects.

Hints and Tips!

This is a list of key ideas (e.g. 'introducing regulations to control some leisure activities'). Try to learn these. In the exam you will earn more marks if you can elaborate the key ideas by giving an example or explanation, e.g. 'allowing power boats on parts of Lake Windermere and Coniston but banning them from Wastwater'.

Glaciation in the Lake District

The Ice Age in Britain lasted from about one million years BP (before the present) to about 20 000 BP. During this time there were several glacial periods, when temperatures fell and ice covered large parts of Britain, separated by inter-glacial periods. In fact, at the moment we may just be in a warm inter-glacial period before the next glaciation starts, and the ice advances again.

During a glacial period the temperature falls by 5–6°C. This means that more snow falls during the winter. In the highlands it does not all melt during the summer. Gradually the snow builds up and covers larger and larger areas with permanent snowfields.

Snow is made up of ice crystals, separated by large volumes of air. As the thickness of the snow cover increases, the lower layers are compressed by the weight above. This squeezes the air out and turns the snow into ice. This ice is much denser and harder than snow.

In some areas, after several decades of build-up of snow and ice, the weight can force the lower layers to start to move and flow out. In highland areas the flowing ice moves downhill, following the valleys. These 'rivers of ice' are called **glaciers**.

Erosion by ice

Before glaciers form there is a period of very cold weather when the rocks are weakened by **freeze–thaw weathering**. This weakens or shatters the rocks. Then the moving ice can erode the rocks in two ways.

DID YOU KNOW?

◆ Imagine making a snowball. You take soft snow and squeeze it to make it firmer. By compressing it you squeeze out the air, and the ice crystals become more compact. This is similar to what happens when snow turns to ice in a glacier.

◆ When water freezes to form ice, its volume increases by about 10%. If water is trapped in cracks in rock this can put great pressure on the rock. After repeated freezing and thawing the rock may finally crack.

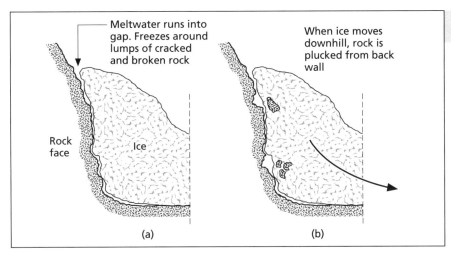

Meltwater runs into gap. Freezes around lumps of cracked and broken rock

When ice moves downhill, rock is plucked from back wall

Rock face

Ice

(a)   (b)

◀ *Figure 3.2 Plucking*

Hints and Tips!

Try to learn these diagrams. Practise drawing them so that you can draw them quickly and accurately in the exam. Examiners give a lot of credit for relevant, well-labelled diagrams.

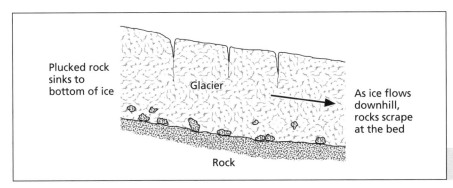

Plucked rock sinks to bottom of ice

Glacier

As ice flows downhill, rocks scrape at the bed

Rock

◀ *Figure 3.3 Abrasion*

These processes form particular physical features.

- **Corries** (called **cwms** in Wales and **cirques** in France) are deep hollows on a mountainside. They have a very steep back wall which is often partly covered by scree. They have a rounded or flat bottom, which may contain a small lake or tarn. There is often a rocky **lip**, where the glacier flowed out of the corrie.

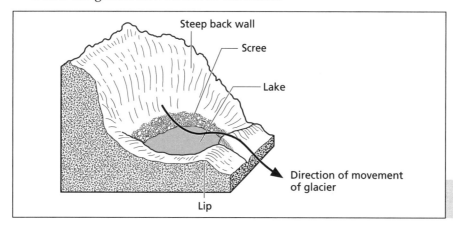

Figure 3.4 Cross-section of a corrie

For example, on the side of Helvellyn in the eastern Lake District there are three large corries, all about 200 metres deep, called Brown Cove, Red Tarn and Nethermost Cove. (Red Tarn is the only one of the three that has a corrie lake.)

- **Arêtes** (or **knife-edge ridges**) are steep-sided ridges of land between two corries. The sides may fall for hundreds of metres, and the tops may be only one or two metres across.

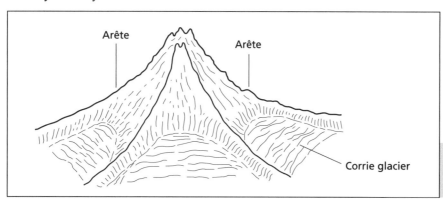

DID YOU KNOW ?

Some people describe corries as 'deep, armchair-shaped hollows'. If this phrase helps you to visualise a corrie, then remember it!

Figure 3.5 Arêtes between a group of corries

On Helvellyn the arête between Brown Cove and Red Tarn is called Swirral Edge. The arête between Red Tarn and Nethermost Cove is called Striding Edge. It is very narrow and steep-sided and is one of the most exciting walks or scrambles in the area.

- **Glacial troughs** (or **U-shaped valleys**) are steep-sided, flat-bottomed valleys. They are usually fairly straight, because the glaciers which eroded them flowed straight, unlike rivers which meander. Some glacial troughs have long, narrow, **ribbon lakes** in them. These were formed mainly by the action of ice deepening the valleys, but also by moraine, deposited when the ice melted, which helped to dam some valleys.

Focus
Point 4

Choose **either** a corrie **or** an arête **or** a U-shaped valley. Explain how plucking and abrasion helped to form your chosen feature.

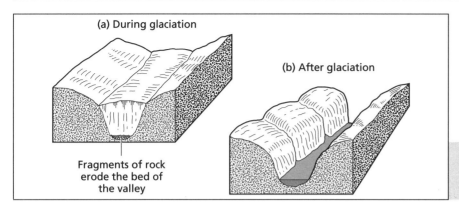

(a) During glaciation

(b) After glaciation

Fragments of rock erode the bed of the valley

◀ *Figure 3.6 U-shaped valley or glaciated trough*

Glenridding Valley and Grisedale lead from the corries on Helvellyn. They both join Ullswater which is the second longest ribbon lake in the Lake District (after Windermere.)

Questions

Learn the names of examples of the features listed above. Use the examples given, or ones that you have studied in class. You should be able to locate them on a map, and describe them.

The attractions of glaciated landscapes

- Most areas where glaciation starts are highlands. This is because temperatures are lower in highlands than in nearby lowlands.

- Highlands are also usually areas of hard rock because hard rock is resistant to erosion. Soft rocks are worn down to form lowlands.

- Because glaciers are mainly found in areas of high land, with hard rock, they produce spectacular scenery.

The valleys were made deep by the ice, but the land in between the valleys resists erosion and forms high peaks. The soil was scraped away from the high land by the ice, leaving the rock exposed, but even this rock is cracked and broken by ice action. This forms steep cliffs and jagged ridges, with flat green valleys in between.

The land in glaciated areas is wild and spectacular, and it attracts many people for outdoor leisure. Some come just to admire the scenery, but it also attracts walkers, rock climbers, skiers, hang-glider pilots, canoeists, mountain bikers, bird watchers, campers, and many others.

Unfortunately, so many people may be attracted that the wild, unspoilt scenery that attracted them may start to be damaged and spoilt!

Increased leisure time and mobility, and pressure on the Parks

Since the Second World War, people in Britain have more leisure time because:

- most working people now have longer periods of paid holiday
- most workers have a shorter working week than they used to

Hints and Tips!

You may be asked to give examples of how glaciated scenery is used for outdoor pursuits. Try to be precise. An answer that says 'Glaciated scenery can be used for walking' will gain some credit. One that says 'Glaciated scenery, like the Striding Edge arête on the side of Helvellyn, can be used for walking' will gain more marks.

- housework is less time-consuming because of labour-saving equipment.

People are also able to travel more easily because:

- far more families now have cars

- the road system has improved with the building of motorways

- networks of inter-city coaches now cover most of the country (although local bus services have declined in many areas).

In addition, the average person has far more 'disposable wealth' (spare money after essential costs have been paid). They have more money to spend on leisure. Many people in cities even have enough money to buy a second home or a caravan in the countryside, just for holiday use.

All this has put great pressure on the countryside, and the Lake District is one of the most seriously affected areas in the UK, because:

- The area has very beautiful scenery.

- It has always been fairly accessible from the densely populated conurbations of Lancashire, Yorkshire and Tyneside.

- The construction of the motorway network in the 1960s and 1970s, with the M6 running very close to the Lakes, made the area even more accessible to a larger number of people.

- The decline of employment in traditional Lakeland occupations like mining and hill farming left many houses abandoned and ready for conversion for tourism or second-home ownership. It also led to a need for diversification of employment, so tourist jobs were welcomed.

The development and management of 'honeypots'

Some of the most difficult problems for the planners in the Lakes have arisen at what are described as 'honeypot' sites. This name arose from the phrase 'they flock there like bees round a honeypot'. In the Lake District honeypots include:

- spectacular scenery for mountain walking, e.g. Helvellyn and the Langdale Pikes

- spectacular scenery accessible by car, e.g. Ashness Bridge near Keswick, and Tarn Hows

- literary links including Beatrix Potter's farm near Hawkshead, and Wordsworth's cottage in Grasmere

- attractive small towns, like Ambleside and Keswick, with their shops, cafés, hotels, museums, lakeside activities and so on

- other attractions, such as the Ravenglass and Eskdale railway and the National Park Centre at Brockholes.

Note that most of these examples have good road links. This is almost essential if a site is to develop into a honeypot. Even Helvellyn and the Langdale Pikes have seriously congested car parks in the valleys below them, and the footpaths to the summits are eroded by walkers.

Of course some people in the UK still work very long hours and have very little leisure time.

ocus Point 5

You may well have visited or studied other honeypot sites. Where do they fit on this list?

Hints and Tips!

This list is an attempt to classify honeypot sites. Putting them in groups like this is a way of making learning easier, and of helping to give a structure to exam answers.

When a site becomes a honeypot, many problems can result, but the tourists can also bring benefits to the local area.

Problems	Benefits
• Litter.	• Trade for local shops.
• Lack of parking spaces, and spread of parked cars onto verges, farmland, etc.	• Money provided for investment in roads, etc.
• Road congestion in the neighbourhood.	• Jobs for local people.
• Lack of toilets.	• Farmers can sell produce such as eggs to visitors.
• Overuse of footpaths leading to erosion of land surface.	• Spare farm buildings can be converted into holiday cottages.
• Conflict with farmers because of tourists damaging hedges, gates, etc.	• B & B guests can be taken in.

Questions

1 Give an example of a honeypot location that you have studied.

2 Describe its attractions.

3 Describe the problems caused by its overuse.

4 Discuss some possible management solutions.

Focus Point 6

Choose one of the honeypot types listed here, or one of your own examples. Make two lists: people who benefit from the existence of the honeypot, and those who suffer.

The issues of second homes, house prices and jobs

In the past, people who lived in villages worked, shopped and carried out their social lives there. The traditional village had a pub, a church, a village hall and a few shops, including a post office and general store. There also had to be a bus service to the local town, because there were not enough people to support a full range of services in the village.

All this changed as the number of second homes and holiday cottages increased. Many houses in the villages are now only lived in at weekends or during the summer; for much of the year they are empty. Meanwhile young people who were born in the village often cannot find work there, or cannot afford to buy homes there because people with jobs in the cities can pay much higher prices for the houses. As house prices increase, local people are forced out and often have to rent council houses in nearby towns.

Local shops and services also suffer from this change. Second-home owners often shop in the city, where prices are much cheaper, so local shops lose trade. Of course they may increase their sales of tourist goods but they can no longer provide the full range of food and household goods. Meanwhile the church, the pub and the village hall lose congregations and customers as the resident population shrinks.

Even the local people come to rely on the town for shopping. More of them have cars and so the bus services lose passengers. In many cases it is only the young, the old and the poor who need to use buses. The number of fare-payers declines, so services are cut. People without cars become more isolated and village life gets more difficult, forcing yet more people to leave.

In the Lake District an attempt has been made to boost public transport by setting up 'post buses'. The postmen who visit the villages use mini-buses and take fare-paying passengers into the towns, but this can only provide a very basic and irregular service at best. Villages continue to lose their services and their sense of identity. The newcomers conserve and improve the houses, but cannot conserve the communities.

However, although the tourists have brought problems to some Lake District communities they have solved others, especially through the jobs they have brought. The tourist industry has now become the biggest employer, by far, in the Lake District. In towns such as Keswick and Ambleside, tourism provides many direct jobs – in hotels, restaurants and information centres, working for the National Park and so on. It also provides many indirect jobs such as:

- shop jobs, in shops made more profitable by the 'tourist spend'
- transport jobs
- farm jobs, which survive because farmers are meeting the 'niche market' for tourists wanting high-quality local products
- building, converting and maintaining tourist accommodation.

Tourism has also brought many benefits to farmers. Not only can they fill the niche markets described above, but they can also diversify into tourist-related businesses (see page 22). They can also receive money from the National Park Authority for conservation work, such as footpath restoration and dry stone wall repair. In fact, as the EU's CAP changes and develops in the next decade or so it seems likely that many Lake District farmers are going to be paid more and more to become 'custodians of the countryside environment' and less and less for producing food which cannot always find a market.

It is to be hoped that a fair balance can be struck between the needs of rural communities and the needs of the urban populations who use the National Park.

People sometimes accuse shops in little tourist villages of charging prices that are far too high. However, they have to do this because the tourist season is only short and the shopkeeper has to make enough profit to survive during the winter.

Questions

Name and describe a village that has been much affected by the growth of second-home ownership.

Exam practice

(a) Give the two main aims of the National Parks when they were first set up.   (1 mark)

(b) (i)   Name one feature in the Lake District that was formed by glacial erosion.   (1 mark)
    (ii) Describe the feature.   (2 marks)
    (iii) Explain how it was formed. You may use a diagram to help your
        explanation.   (5 marks)

(c) (i)   What is a 'honeypot' site?   (1 mark)
    (ii) Name an example of a honeypot site in the Lake District.   (1 mark)
    (iii) Describe two problems caused by visitors to honeypot sites and the areas
        around them.   (4 marks)

Hints and Tips!

This chapter was about glaciation. The previous chapter was about farming in the Lake District. You should think about how they are linked. For instance:

- Glaciers scraped soil off the hillsides, leaving only thin, stony soils, which are quite fertile but poorly drained

- Some glaciers deposited soil on the valley bottoms, leaving soils which are quite fertile but poorly drained

- Arêtes and corrie back walls are steep and can be dangerous places for sheep and shepherds

- Glaciated valleys can make good route-ways – like the valley and Dunmail Raise between Ambleside and Keswick

If you can make points like these in the exam, you could earn high level marks.

4 Electricity generation for the future

For this topic you should study:

- the location of power stations (gas, coal, HEP and nuclear) and wind farms, and reasons for the locations
- advantages and disadvantages of each type of power station, including impact on the environment
- reasons for the development of alternative power sources: wind and solar.

If you look ahead to chapter 5, The changing location of manufacturing industry or to chapter 6, Understanding the modern urban environment, you will see that the development of electricity in the twentieth century has had an enormous effect on many aspects of our life. When electricity replaced coal as the major source of power in industry, it allowed factory location to become far more 'footloose'. Entrepreneurs were no longer tied to locations on the coalfields or close to ports and railways.

Electricity is a very easily transportable form of power. Yet when power stations which generate electricity are being built, great care has to be taken over their location. Most power stations are not at all footloose.

Location of thermal power stations

Coal-fired stations	
• Must be near large supplies of coal because it is bulky and very expensive to transport.	• Often linked to pits by special loop railways that only carry coal.
• Need large amounts of cooling water.	• Built along major rivers, especially the Trent and the Aire in the Notts/Yorks areas.
• Must be large for economies of scale.	• Only built in ideal locations.

Most of the coal used now comes either from imports or from open cast mines. The UK produces little deep-mined coal. Present coal-fired power stations will be kept open but new ones will only be opened if they are less polluting than traditional coal-fired power stations.

Gas-fired stations	
• Need access to gas – but it is the most easily transportable source of fuel.	• The most footloose of all thermal power sources.
	• Should be close to a gas pipeline terminal.

Small and medium-sized stations are economic. The 'dash for gas' in the late 1980s/90s led to the building of several new stations. More may follow.

Hints and Tips!

You should know at least two factors that influence the location of each type of power station.

ocus Point 1

Cover up the pages. Name one example of each of the following types of power station:

- nuclear
- HEP
- coal-fired
- gas-fired.

Describe the location of each example. Give the reasons for each of the locations you have described.

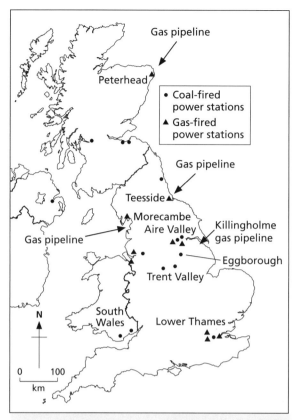

▲ *Figure 4.1 Some coal-fired power stations and recently-built gas-fired power stations*

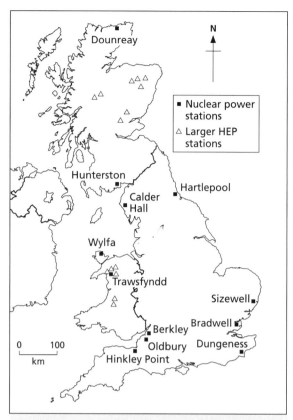

▲ *Figure 4.2 Some of Britain's nuclear power stations and larger HEP stations*

Nuclear power stations

- Need large areas of flat land, underlain by stable rocks.
- Need very large amounts of cooling water.

- Were originally built away from dense population, because of risk during development.
- The risk is no longer so great, but there is still much opposition.

- All on the coast, except Trawsfynnydd, which is on a lake.
- Were originally in isolated areas of the north and west, but later plants were nearer the cities.
- Any new plants will probably be built fairly close to the market, i.e. the conurbations.

The cost of development of new power stations is very great. So is the cost of closing old ones. It is unlikely that any new plants will be built in the next ten years at least.

HEP stations

- Need a large and reliable supply of water: heavy rainfall and low evaporation.
- Suitable sites for reservoirs: stable impermeable rock, cheap, sparsely populated land to flood.
- Need a large 'head' of water.
- Land of low landscape value preferred.

- Highlands in north and west.

- Few suitable large rivers in UK highlands.
- Rules out most areas in National Parks.

There are very few potential sites with streams big enough to make investment worthwhile. Little scope for further development.

 __estions

> Refer to examples of power stations that you have studied.
> How do the factors described above fit your case studies?

Advantages and disadvantages of different forms of power stations

Renewable or non-renewable

- HEP is renewable.

- Nuclear power uses only very small amounts of raw materials, and it is possible to recycle and re-use spent nuclear fuel.

- All fossil fuels are non-renewable, but:

  Coal – there are large supplies left but they are deep and therefore difficult, expensive and dangerous to mine.

  Gas – is often found with oil. Some is piped to houses but in the past much was burnt off as waste. There has been a recent rush to build gas-powered power stations. North Sea supplies may only last for about 20 years. Imports can replace it after that, but gas supplies will not last for ever.

Impact on the environment

Positive	Negative
HEP	
• Does not cause any air pollution. • It does not produce waste.	• Dams in highland valleys cause visual pollution. • Land is lost when valleys flood, but is usually of low agricultural value.
Nuclear	
• Does not produce CO_2, which contributes to global warming. • Does not produce sulphur and nitrogen oxides, which contribute to acid rain.	• Nuclear waste is dangerous and difficult to dispose of safely. It can remain toxic for many decades. There is much fear of spills and accidents, although the safety record of the UK's nuclear industry is good. Safety costs are very high. This form of power is still being developed and long-term effects are not completely understood.
Coal	
• Coal power has been used for a long time, so it is well understood.	• Releases carbon dioxide which is the biggest cause of the greenhouse effect and global warming.

Hints and Tips!

Questions often ask about the advantages and disadvantages of the various types of power station. The issues are complicated. No one type of power has all the advantages. None has all the disadvantages. Try hard to write a fair and balanced answer.

Fitting 'scrubbers' to the chimneys of coal-fired power stations can remove almost all the sulphur which causes acid rain. However, if they were fitted to all the UK's coal-fired power stations it would add 10% to our electricity bills. Is it worth the cost?

Positive	Negative
Coal cont.	
• New technology means emissions of damaging gases can be reduced – but at a cost.	• Burning releases sulphur and nitrogen oxides, which are the main cause of acid rain. • Mining and transport of coal also causes environmental damage.
Gas	
• Much cleaner and less polluting than coal or oil. • No problem of waste disposal like nuclear has.	• Produces some carbon dioxide, but far less than coal or oil.

Relative costs

It is very difficult to obtain figures for the relative costs of the different forms of power generation. Probably, in terms of cost per unit of energy, the five main sources can be put in this order:

Cheapest ——————————————————→ Most expensive

Gas   Wind   Coal   HEP   Oil   Nuclear

Employment prospects

In any discussion of energy supplies, the size of the workforce has to be considered. Modern electricity generation is very capital intensive. Modern power stations cost enormous sums to build, but they are very mechanised so they only employ a small labour force. However ...

● Coal mining employed hundreds of thousands of men up to the 1960s. Now it employs fewer than 20 000. If any more coal-fired power stations are closed the mining industry will shrink even further.

● Nuclear power stations make a big contribution to employment in some areas. Sellafield in west Cumbria is the major employer in an area with few other sources of employment, except tourism.

● New gas-fired power stations need a very small workforce.

What can be done to reduce the threat of global warming?

Most world leaders now accept that global warming is a threat, and that something needs to be done about it. It seems certain that responsibility for action will lie mainly with the more economically developing countries (MEDCs). They have been, and still are, the main polluters. In addition, they can better afford to bring in the changes. There are two different types of response to the threat.

1   Plan now to reduce the damaging effects of warming.

2   Try to slow down warming by controlling greenhouse gases.

Hints and Tips!

In many coalfield areas the closure of the pits still makes people very angry. If you are angry about a topic it is quite acceptable to let your anger show in a geography answer – as long as you support your arguments with clear facts and figures.

Global warming results from the greenhouse effect, which is caused mainly by emissions of carbon dioxide. It may lead to rises in sea-level. Do not confuse it with the destruction of the ozone layer, which is mainly caused by CFC emissions.

1   *How can we plan to reduce the effects of warming?*

Even the most optimistic forecasts for the reduction of emissions accept that some warming will still happen. Therefore the problem must be managed. This means that, over the next 50 years or so:

- People must plan to control floods caused by rising sea-levels. The Thames Barrage is one example of this being done, but the problems of places like Bangladesh are on a far larger scale. The Bangladeshi government, with aid from the World Bank, is spending hundreds of millions of dollars on the Flood Action Plan. This is a series of embankments along the coast and river banks in the Ganges delta region.

- People must plan for water supplies in areas where drought might be caused by climate change. Already the UK has suffered water shortages in several areas. Even wet countries like ours need to introduce very efficient national water grids, so that resources can be used efficiently.

- People should attempt to 'drought-proof' agriculture. The development of strains of plants which use less water is probably important. More important is to develop techniques of farming that use water less wastefully. Conservation of water, like conservation of energy, will become more and more important.

The management of resources should be based on planning for sustainable development in all parts of the world.

2   *How can warming be prevented or slowed down?*

- At the Earth Summit in 1992 it was agreed that countries should reduce emissions of greenhouse gases to 1990 levels by 2010. Many, but not all, countries agreed to this.

- The Kyoto conference in 1997 tried to persuade countries to go further than this, and to start cutting emissions now. Europe and Japan promised to do so. The USA refused to sign the Kyoto agreement. They said that it would lead to far too many job losses.

- The main way to reduce emissions is to reduce the burning of coal and oil. To help this people can:
  - use more renewable energy (see 'Development of alternative power sources' below)
  - use more natural gas, which emits less carbon than coal does
  - conserve energy in the home and in industry
  - plan transport policies to reduce the use of cars and lorries.

Development of alternative power sources

At the moment some attempts are being made to develop alternative sources of energy. None of these is commercially viable on a large scale yet, but at some time during the twenty-first century it will become essential to use one or more of these alternatives to produce most of our energy.

As fossil fuels become more scarce, the price of energy will rise. This will mean that research and development of alternative sources will

Greenhouse gases let the sun's rays into the earth's surface, but trap the heat and do not allow it to escape. This leads to global warming.

ocus Point 2

Cover up the page. List four ways that countries/people can reduce the use of coal and oil, and so help reduce global warming.

become more and more profitable. Now there are many ideas about possible ways of producing energy and the increased price will make development of these sources profitable. Unless they are developed, the developed economies may collapse.

The following are possible sources of the alternative energy supplies:

Wind – Wind-powered turbines have been built in many areas of highland and coastal Britain. Individual turbines can provide power for small, isolated communities. However, most developments in the last ten years or so have been wind farms with groups of between three and twenty-five turbines each. The improvements in technology coupled with taxes on more polluting forms of electricity generation mean that wind power has become one of the cheapest ways of generating electricity.

Most of the wind farms are:

- in the west of the country, facing the prevailing winds

- on high land, where the wind is stronger (although some are also built on low land near the coast, where the wind blows off the sea)

- at the top of smoothly rounded hills – because crags and cliffs make the wind turbulent, and so less efficient

- at least 1km from the nearest house and at least 2km from the nearest village, to avoid disturbing people

- close to a road or track, for access for building and maintenance.

Wind power does not produce any polluting gases, but it can damage the environment. The windiest places are often on hilltops in beautiful areas, and wind turbines can ruin the scenery.

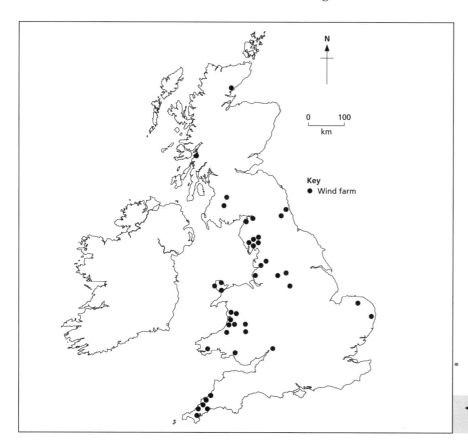

◀ Figure 4.3 Sites of wind farms in Britain

However, experimental wind farms have been built out at sea. To date, turbines have been erected off the Mersey estuary and off Blyth in north-east England. It seems likely that there will be a big expansion of off-shore generation, mainly because there is likely to be far less opposition to such developments.

Solar power – The sun provides an enormous amount of energy to Earth. If this could be harnessed it would meet most of our needs. Some houses have been fitted with solar panels to heat water. If this can be stored it can be an important source of energy on a small scale.

Most people are familiar with solar power on an even smaller scale: you may well have a calculator powered by a solar cell, which uses the sun's energy to produce electricity. Some cars have even been powered by experimental solar cells. This seems to be a very important area of research. In future, technology could be developed to use solar cells to generate a large proportion of our energy needs.

Questions

Choose one wind farm that you have studied. Describe:
- its site and the reason for the choice of that site
- the advantages and disadvantages of the scheme for the local area and the country as a whole.

Exam practice

(a) On a map of the UK, mark and name:
  (i) an area where coal is important for the generation of electricity
  (ii) an area where HEP generation is important
  (iii) a nuclear power station
  (iv) an area that may well be useful for generating electricity from an alternative energy source. (4 marks)

(b) Give two reasons why the area you marked for (i) above is suitable for coal-fired power stations. (4 marks)

(c) Give two reasons why the area you marked for (ii) above is suitable for HEP generation. (4 marks)

(d) Nuclear power stations were originally built in remote parts of the country, but later ones have been built near to areas of dense population. Explain why. (4 marks)

(e) Why is the government encouraging research into the development of alternative power resources, such as wind and solar power? (4 marks)

5 The changing location of manufacturing industry

For this topic you should study:

- manufacturing industry as a system, with reference to:
  - inputs, processes and outputs
  - the influence of raw materials, fuel supplies, labour supply, transport, markets and government policy
  - a chemicals industry on a river estuary
  - modern industry along the M4 corridor.

Factors affecting industrial location

The simplest definition of manufacturing industry says that it 'takes raw materials and processes them to make finished products'. Really it is rather more complicated than this. Few factories take an item through the full process from raw material to finished product. Some factories use raw materials and process them. Then the product of that factory may be taken somewhere else to be made into parts, which are then used in an assembly plant to make finished products.

However, all factories have inputs which they process to produce outputs.

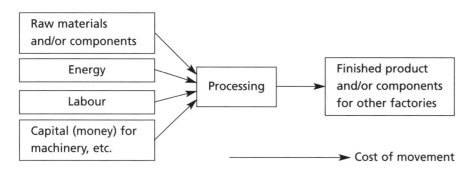

ocus Point 1

Cover up the diagram.

Name four types of input that go into any factory.

Give two names to describe the outputs of factories.

Every entrepreneur who builds a factory tries to choose the best possible site. This is the place where the factory can make most profit. One way of increasing profit is to increase sales, by being near a good market. Another way is to reduce costs. Geographers are especially interested in how costs can be reduced by cutting transport costs. Ways of reducing costs include building at or close to:

(1) mines, etc. which supply energy or raw materials

(2) railway stations, ports, motorway junctions, etc. where transport is cheaper

(3) areas with high unemployment, which have a cheaper labour force

(4) a well-trained labour force (cheaper training costs)

(5) areas where government subsidies are available (which are often areas of high unemployment)

(6) areas of dense population where there is a large market.

No location offers all the factors listed above, but different types of factory have different needs. For instance:

- An iron and steel works uses large amounts of iron ore and coal, so (1) would be very important for its location.

- A soft drinks canning plant does not use much raw material, because the main ingredient is water, so factor (1) is not important. However, the finished product is bulky, so it needs to cut transport costs for the finished product. Factor (6) is important.

In the two studies that follow – the chemicals industry and high-tech industry – you should keep the six factors listed above in your mind at all times. They help to explain the very different location patterns of the two industries.

Hints and Tips!

Try to learn this list. You will probably not get a question that asks you to write out such a list, but it can provide a very good starting point for planning answers to questions on industrial location.

The chemicals industry on river estuaries
There are five river estuaries in England where major chemicals industries have developed. They are shown on the map to the right.

They all have the following features in common:

- They have easy access for large bulk-carrying ships.

- Oil refining has developed along each estuary.

- They all have flat, low-lying land on which to build large industrial complexes.

- They are well served by road transport.

- They are close to large urban areas which provide a labour force and a market.

However, the three more southerly areas have always relied almost completely on imported raw materials. Both Merseyside and Teesside originally developed because of local supplies of raw materials, and these are still important today.

Both areas are also near to coalfields which used to provide both energy and raw materials.

The nature of modern chemicals industries
The chemicals industry in some areas has been described as resembling a 'spaghetti bowl'. The tangle of long strands of spaghetti is represented by the tangle of pipelines which connect the various plants.

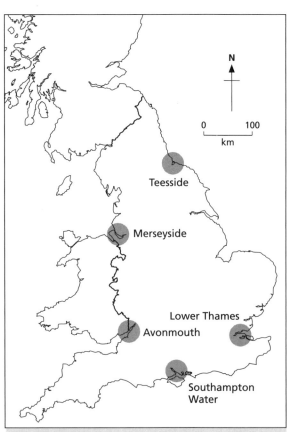

▲ Figure 5.1 Major estuaries with chemicals industries

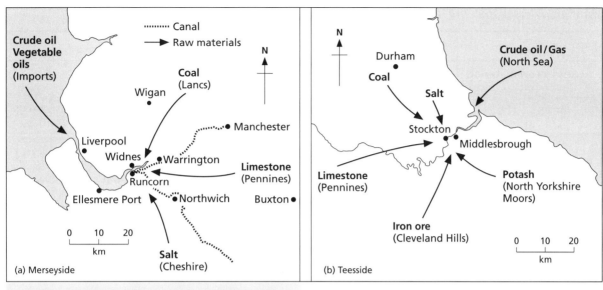

▲ *Figure 5.2 Raw materials for the chemicals industry (a) Merseyside   (b) Teesside*

Essentially what happens in the modern chemicals industry is:

- raw materials consisting of complex chemical mixtures and compounds are taken and broken down
- different chemicals are separated from each other
- chemicals are reassembled to make new products.

The heavy chemicals industry uses large amounts of a few raw materials, and makes products for other industries. The light chemicals industry recombines those products into a variety of carefully designed products to meet precise market needs.

For instance, consider two products of the chemicals industry, plastics and pharmaceutical products (or medical drugs). Both come in an enormous range of products. Plastics can be clear or opaque, rigid or flexible, and biodegradable or non-biodegradable, and so on. Each special product is designed for a different purpose and needs a slightly different combination of the same chemical elements.

Pharmaceuticals are equally complex and varied. They range from common, rather old-fashioned drugs like aspirin and indigestion remedies to very sophisticated chemicals to treat cancers and AIDS or to prevent rejection of transplanted organs.

Hints and Tips!

There are many similarities between these two areas and Europort in the Netherlands (see chapter 10). If you study Europort, study the two areas together. It makes it easier to learn both of them.

Why are Merseyside and Teesside good locations?

	Merseyside	**Teesside**
Access to raw materials	Local salt, limestone	Local salt, limestone, potash
Port facilities	Deepwater Mersey estuary.	Deepwater Tees estuary.
	Imports of oil etc.	Imports of oil etc. + pipelines from North Sea oil and gas fields.
Road links	M56, M6, M62 form a network around the area.	No motorway link to national motorway network but reasonable network of A roads.
Energy	Close to Lancashire coalfield. Used to be important, but now electricity provides main power.	Close to Durham coalfield. Used to be important. Now has gas-fired power stations, using North Sea gas.
Labour supply	High unemployment so cheap workforce is available.* Long tradition of chemicals industry, so skilled workforce available.	
Government incentives	Development areas, so aid available for building, equipping factories, training workers, tax reduction, etc.	
Capital	Local firms with long-standing links and investments in the area.	
Markets	Local textile and engineering industries provide markets. Easy access to Lancashire and Midlands conurbations. Local ports and airports for export.	Local engineering, mining industry etc. provides a market. Fairly easy access to Tyneside and Yorkshire conurbations. Local port and airport for export. Faces EU across North Sea

* Note that the chemicals industry is very capital intensive. It has a fairly small workforce compared with the large amount invested in capital and equipment. Most of the workforce are highly skilled and trained, so the presence of a cheap, unskilled workforce is not a very important factor.

Unfortunately, in recent years the chemical industry in this country has changed a great deal. Teesside, in particular, has suffered from these changes. Three factors have hit the area:

- demand for many of the heavy chemicals has fallen, and Teesside used to specialise in these products

- research into new chemical products has increased rapidly. Unfortunately much of the research is located in other parts of the country, especially in south-east England

- competition from other countries with lower costs, especially lower labour costs, has reduced the market for bulk chemicals from this country.

Teesside and Merseyside became two of the country's worst unemployment blackspots in the 1980s. Government initiatives, such as Urban Development Corporations, brought new jobs in the 1990s. However, the chemical industries will never again be the mass employers that they once were. In fact, the new, diversified economies will probably be healthier in the long run.

Hints and Tips!

Learn the layout of the table. The side headings provide a good structure to help you learn the details. Also note where the same idea can be applied to **both** examples. This saves time and effort when you are revising.

High-technology industry in the M4 corridor

The raw materials used to make a computer are only worth a few pounds, but the actual cost of a computer may be well over a thousand pounds. The money pays for:

- the highly educated designers and programmers who developed the computer and its component parts, such as micro-chips and processors – in other words, **research and development (R&D)** costs

- the cost of developing the software

- the skilled labour that made the components, and then assembled them

- the cost of plant and machinery in the factories

- advertising and promotion

- transport of the very fragile finished product

- sales staff, and the after-sales technical back-up staff.

This all goes to show that the old rules of industrial location do not apply to modern, high-tech industry. Computer manufacture does not have to be located where the raw materials are imported, or near to a coal mine. Instead, industries like this are located in two types of area: the work is often split between 'development' sites and 'assembly' sites.

Development sites need:

- access to highly educated, creative thinkers, who are usually found in and around universities

- an attractive environment, where these workers will be willing to work

- contact with other people in high-tech industry, who can share ideas and stimulate further development work

- easy access to the rest of the world (via airports) so that ideas can be shared (potential buyers and providers of components and programs can easily keep in contact too)

- good road access, by fast, uncongested routes.

Assembly sites need:

- skilled and semi-skilled workers with reasonably low wage rates

- government subsidies (if possible) which are usually paid to firms that locate in 'development areas' with high unemployment

- easy contact with the development sites, and with the market – good road access is essential.

Figure 5.3 on page 46 shows the development that has taken place along the M4 and around the M25 to the west of London. There has also been development north-east of London, along the M11. These three areas combined all the factors needed for the growth of the research and development sector of high-tech industry. Once established in this area, high-tech industries multiplied.

The Cambridge Science Park, linked to the university, is probably the UK's best example.

ocus Points 2 and 3

◆ Go through this list linking each point to a specific fact about the M4 Corridor on the map on page 46. In other words, link the theory to a real-life example.

◆ Several assembly plants developed in small towns in South Wales and Central Scotland. Why were a lot of workers available here? Which declining industries had they come from?

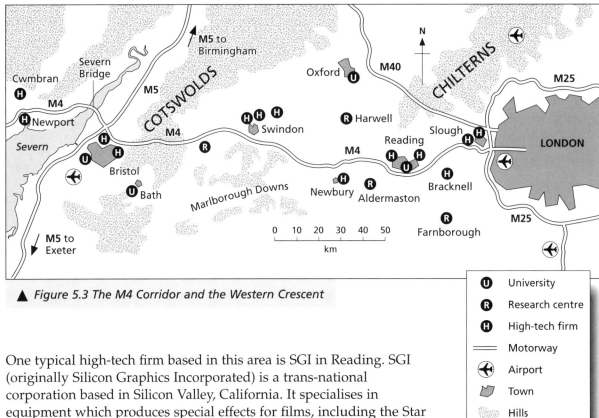

▲ *Figure 5.3 The M4 Corridor and the Western Crescent*

Legend:
- **U** University
- **R** Research centre
- **H** High-tech firm
- Motorway
- ✈ Airport
- Town
- Hills

One typical high-tech firm based in this area is SGI in Reading. SGI (originally Silicon Graphics Incorporated) is a trans-national corporation based in Silicon Valley, California. It specialises in equipment which produces special effects for films, including the Star Wars movies, and virtual reality displays for industry. These help designers and engineers to plan processes and new models. For instance, car designers can build virtual models of their cars at the design stage, and oil well engineers can test ways of drilling down to oil reservoirs to make sure that all possible reserves are removed.

SGI built their European headquarters in Reading and these are the main reasons that their spokesperson gave for that choice.

- Reading is not London! It is close to the capital but prices for premises and housing for workers are a lot cheaper than in London.

- Communications are excellent, with the M4 for links to the key areas of the UK, and Heathrow nearby for links to the USA and the world.

- The synergy we feel from being close to so many other firms in the ICT, high-tech sector. We compete for workers, but this exchange means lots of new ideas whizzing around.

- Good universities and research institutes nearby.

- A beautiful environment nearby which makes the area attractive to the workforce, including many foreign workers, who could have their pick of anywhere in the world.

Questions

The M4 Corridor is an important area for the development of the ICT industry.

1 Name a town that you have studied where the ICT industry is important.

2 Describe the industry that has developed there.

3 Explain the factors that attracted it to that area.

Exam practice

(a) (i) Give two reasons why industry often develops around river estuaries. (2 marks)

(ii) Name three river estuaries in the UK where large chemicals industries
have developed. (3 marks)

(b) For one of the estuaries named in (a) (ii) above:

(i) Name one raw material that is (or was) mined locally. (1 mark)

(ii) Name a place where that raw material was mined. (1 mark)

(iii) Name a raw material that is imported by ship. (1 mark)

(iv) Name a town close to the estuary where the chemicals industry is important. (1 mark)

(c) Explain why many chemical plants are often found grouped close together in a
small area. Use examples to illustrate the points you make in your answer. (5 marks)

(d) Why has the M4 Corridor developed as the main centre for high-tech industry
in the UK? (6 marks)

6 Understanding the modern urban environment

For this topic you should study:
- the growth and morphology of **one** large urban area in the UK
- the processes leading to the development of a conurbation
- the causes and effects of inner city decline
- the process of urban renewal
- development on the rural-urban fringe: suburbanisation, counterurbanisation, commuter villages
- the changing location of the retail trade: out-of-town shopping centres and retail parks and their effect on the high street
- the impact of road transport on urban structure and environment. Possible solutions to the problems of traffic in towns.

In this section of the specification you will have studied the growth, characteristics and morphology (or the layout) of one town or city – probably the one that you live in or close to. Your teacher probably chose this because you were already quite familiar with the area. **But** do not let familiarity breed contempt. You need to work hard on learning the relevant geography about your local town. Revise this topic as much as any other.

You need to know:

- where was the **site** of the settlement (the place where it was originally built)?

- what is the **situation** of the settlement (its position in relation to the area and the other settlements surrounding it)?

- what were its original **functions** and how have its functions changed over time, through to the present day?

- what is its **morphology**? (How have its urban zones developed over time? How do they link together now?)

You have probably studied some models of urban morphology. You probably recognise the Burgess model and the Hoyt model.

Both of these are useful in helping to understand how towns developed in the first half of the twentieth century. Since then, though, things have become more complicated, largely because of the influence of roads and new forms of transport. Figure 6.2 is an updated version of the Hoyt model.

Hints and Tips!

Think about your main urban area case study. Learn to draw a simple, 30-second sketch map to show the original site factors.

Then learn to draw a 45-second sketch map to show its situation.

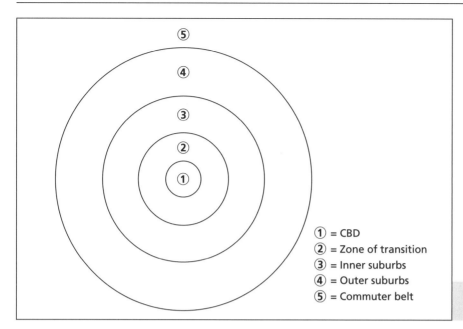

① = CBD
② = Zone of transition
③ = Inner suburbs
④ = Outer suburbs
⑤ = Commuter belt

◀ *Figure 6.1 The Burgess model*

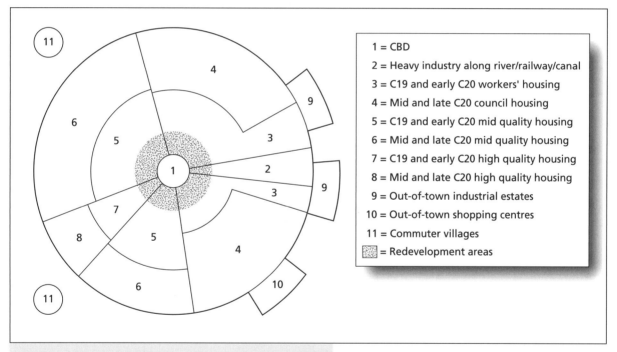

1 = CBD
2 = Heavy industry along river/railway/canal
3 = C19 and early C20 workers' housing
4 = Mid and late C20 council housing
5 = C19 and early C20 mid quality housing
6 = Mid and late C20 mid quality housing
7 = C19 and early C20 high quality housing
8 = Mid and late C20 high quality housing
9 = Out-of-town industrial estates
10 = Out-of-town shopping centres
11 = Commuter villages
▨ = Redevelopment areas

▲ *Figure 6.2 A model of urban structures in UK towns*

These models must be related to your own case study of an urban area. You need to make copies of them (or use tracing overlays) which you can relate to places in your own area. For instance:

• where is the centre of the CBD?

• where is the edge of the CBD?

• where is the transition zone in your town?

Name parts of this zone where the CBD is spreading outwards. Name parts where housing or industry is run down, forming a 'twilight zone'.

- where is/was the old industrial zone?

- what factors attracted the old industry there?

- where were the houses built for the workers in that industrial zone?

- where were the houses built for workers in the services in the CBD?

- where were the areas of early twentieth century middle-class housing?

- how has housing in the two zones above changed in the late twentieth century?
  Did it improve (gentrification)?
  Did it become run down and need redevelopment?

- where were the estates of council housing built for low-income groups in the mid to late twentieth century?

- where were the estates of houses built for middle-income, owner occupiers in this same period?

- where were the really expensive houses built at this time?

- where are the commuter villages?

- where are the out-of-town shopping centres?

- where is the new industrial development?

The development of conurbations

As the industrial towns were growing in the nineteenth and early twentieth centuries, there were few planning regulations to control their spread. Individual settlements developed in a random way as entrepreneurs built factories and houses in the places that were cheapest and most convenient. A number of factors caused towns to spread.

- Industry spread along the banks of rivers, and along railway lines.

- As road transport developed, towns spread along main roads, in a process called **ribbon development**.

- It is cheaper to build on new sites than to clear old buildings away and reclaim used land. The development of **greenfield sites** on the edges of towns caused the built-up areas to spread.

All these processes helped to cause the development of **conurbations**. This term was first used in 1915 to describe South Lancashire. Towns and cities including Manchester, Salford, Oldham, Bury, Rochdale, Bolton and others had all spread outwards and started to merge, especially along the main roads, railways and canals. They did not form a continuous built-up area. There were still patches of park, farmland, woodland, etc. around all these towns, but the urban sprawl around the edges of towns was threatening the few remaining open areas.

ocus Point 1

Think of an area in your case study town which illustrates each of the ideas in this list.

Hints and Tips!

Learn this definition: 'A conurbation is found where several towns and/or cities have spread until they merge and form a single, large urban area.'

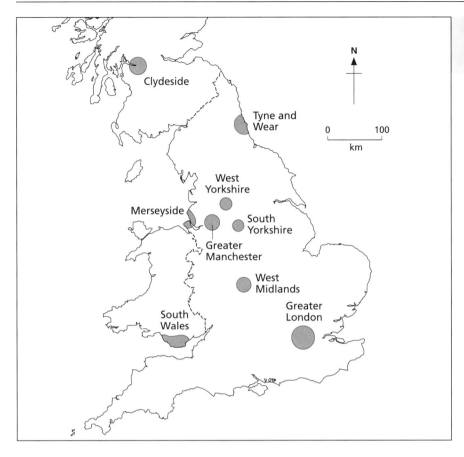

◀ *Figure 6.3*
Conurbations in Great Britain

Other conurbations developed in Central Scotland, Tyne and Wear, West Yorkshire, Merseyside, the Potteries, West Midlands, South Wales, Greater London and along the south coast. Some geographers even suggest that a 'super-conurbation' is developing which stretches from Preston in the north-west to Dover in the south-east!

Since 1945 planning regulations have tried to limit the spread of conurbations in the UK. Local planning controls and Green Belts have been imposed to try to conserve areas of open countryside around the edges of the main built-up areas. Since the mid-1980s a lot of funding has been put into inner city areas to try to attract development back there, and to reduce the pressure on the urban fringes.

Some geographers would go even further. They talk about **Europolis**, a conurbation which stretches from the English conurbations across the Channel to include Rotterdam and other built-up areas in the Netherlands, the Ruhr conurbation in Germany, parts of Belgium, and northern and eastern France! Look for this area in an atlas.

Questions

Draw a sketch map of a conurbation that you have studied. Mark and name:
- the main towns and cities
- places where built-up areas have merged
- areas of open space in between the spreading settlements
- the Green Belt, if it exists in that conurbation.

Inner city decline

The inner city areas of the industrial towns were built to suit nineteenth-century conditions. By the middle of the twentieth century they had become serious problem areas. The problems included the following.

- Slum housing – this was often poorly built and very crowded.

- Lack of open space – housing was crowded with no room for private gardens or public open space in inner city housing areas.

- Air pollution – coal-powered factories, houses heated with coal and fumes from transport all pollute the air, causing lung diseases.

- Traffic congestion – the volume of vehicles increased on roads built before the days of mass car ownership and lorry transport.

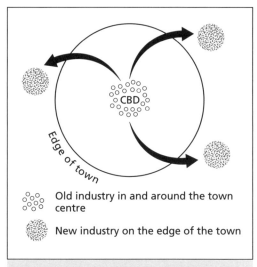

Old industry in and around the town centre

New industry on the edge of the town

▲ Figure 6.4 Movement of industry out of towns

The movement of industry from the inner cities

After about 1930 transport by lorry started to become very important for some industries, especially the new, light industries. The owners of the new factories wanted to avoid the crowded, old industrial areas. Many new factories were built along main roads leading out of the town centres. The new buildings were usually lighter and more spacious than the old factories. They were built fairly close to the new suburban housing that was spreading outwards at this time.

As road transport became more and more important, new factories were built further from the centres. Many were built on industrial estates at the edges of towns and cities.

Advantages of industrial estates	Disadvantages of inner city industrial sites
• Easy access to motorways, ring roads and by-passes.	• Congested, with narrow roads built for smaller lorries and less road traffic.
• A clean, attractive environment, close to open countryside and fresh air.	• Old buildings in a noisy and often polluted environment.
• Land is usually cheap.	• Land is more expensive because of restricted area.
• 'Greenfield sites' do not need expensive work to make them fit for new building.	• Old 'brownfield' sites often need expensive demolition and reclamation before new building can take place.

Housing change in inner cities

Many people have moved out from inner cities since 1930. At the same time there has been much redevelopment of inner city housing.

1 **Slum clearance** – many large areas of old terraced housing which had become unfit for human habitation have been knocked down. Much of this old housing was built in the nineteenth century and lacked basic amenities like inside toilets, hot and cold running water and damp-proofing.

ocus
Point 2

Cover up this table. Give three reasons why industry has moved from inner cities to industrial estates on the edges of built-up areas.

2 **High-rise housing** was built to replace the slum housing. Many residential tower blocks were built between about 1950 and 1975. This was a fairly cheap way to provide housing with all modern facilities. Unfortunately the flats were often badly built and suffered from condensation, expensive heating systems, vandalism, broken lifts, isolation of people in the flats, etc. They were often unpopular, and many of these flats have either been demolished or redesigned without the higher floors.

3 **Low-rise/high-density housing** was built later. Such housing had to be quite compact, because the land was expensive, but it was designed to give people privacy. The estates were designed with large areas of public open space. These open areas caused many problems because no one had responsibility for them.

4 **Housing regeneration** By the 1980s the worst slums had been cleared from most towns and cities. It became possible to improve the remaining housing without knocking it down. It is cheaper to keep old houses and add kitchens, bathrooms, fire escapes, new roofs, damp-proof courses, etc. Such work does not destroy communities. It causes less social disruption than the old slum clearance and redevelopment.

> **Note** At the end of the First World War, many politicians talked about knocking down the slums and building new houses for the soldiers coming home from the trenches. These would be 'Homes fit for heroes'. Unfortunately many of the old slums were not demolished until the 1960s.

Pushes from inner cities	Pulls to suburbs
• Housing was old and run-down.	• New, better-designed housing.
• Land was expensive, so houses were small.	• Land was cheaper, so houses could be larger.
• Little space for gardens or car parking.	• Plenty of space for gardens and car parking.
• Roads congested.	• New roads, designed for mass car ownership.
• Noisy and polluted by industry and traffic.	• Cleaner, greener environment.
• Social problems increased: crime, drugs, prostitution, etc.	• Fewer, less obvious social problems.
• Increasing unemployment as industry left.	• Increased employment as industry moved in.
• Shops and services left the inner city as people moved out and out-of-town shopping increased.	• Many new services and shopping centres built in suburbs and out-of-town locations.

Industrial renewal in the inner cities

In 1981 Mrs Thatcher (then the Prime Minister) visited an area of industrial dereliction in Middlesborough. This was an area where a lot of heavy industry had closed down. (See page 44.) She set up the Urban Development Corporations (UDCs) to try to bring new industry and commerce to areas of industrial decline. Teesside had its own UDC. Other UDCs were in London's Docklands, the Trafford area of Manchester and Salford, Sheffield, Tyneside and Wearside.

The UDCs were given the tasks of:

- clearing industrial dereliction, especially contaminated land

- up-dating the infrastructure of roads, water supply, sewers, telecommunication networks, etc.

> **Note** You need to know which of these ideas about industrial renewal apply to an area near you. If your town does not have a UDC try to find about other ways that it has tried to attract industry and commerce.

- encouraging private firms to locate in UDC areas by:
  - offering tax and rates reductions
  - helping to provide opportunities to train the labour force
  - building-up the image of the area
  - providing ready-built premises for rent.

- encouraging the improvement of housing that was already in the area, and the building of new housing, where needed, at prices that were suitable for the workforce that was needed.

Patterns of housing in towns and cities

Geography students need to understand where different types of housing are found. Housing often changes as one moves away from the city centre towards the edge. In general terms the pattern is like this:

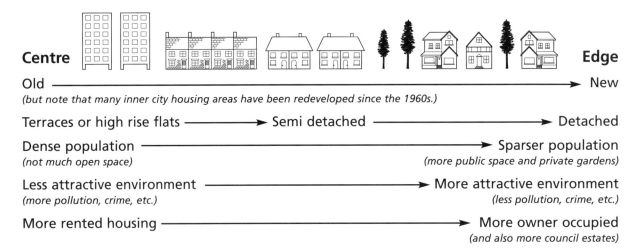

Centre   **Edge**

Old ———————————————————————————————→ New
(but note that many inner city housing areas have been redeveloped since the 1960s.)

Terraces or high rise flats ———→ Semi detached ——————→ Detached

Dense population ———————————————————→ Sparser population
(not much open space)   *(more public space and private gardens)*

Less attractive environment ———————————————→ More attractive environment
(more pollution, crime, etc.)   *(less pollution, crime, etc.)*

More rented housing ————————————————————→ More owner occupied
                                                 (and also more council estates)

Questions

1 For your case study town or city, describe the types of housing found in named examples of:
   - inner city areas
   - inner suburbs
   - outer suburbs
   - rural–urban fringe.

2 Some people say 'The quality of housing in towns improves as you move from the centre to the edges'. Is this hypothesis true in your case study town?

3 Some cities are described as having **concentric rings** of housing types. Others have **sectors**. Does your case study fit either of these models?

Population movement in the industrial towns

(a) Decline in inner city population

The figures below show how Manchester's population has changed. They are typical of what happened in many towns and cities in the UK.

Manchester's population

Year	Total population
1931	766 311
1951	703 082
1961	662 021
1971	543 859
1981	462 500
1991	438 500
1996	430 818

◆There has been a census in Britain once every 10 years from 1801 to the present, except in 1941 when the country was at war.

◆Note that the population of Manchester fell by almost 120 000 (about 18%) in just 10 years after 1961. This was the peak period for slum clearance in the inner city.

There were two main reasons for the changes.

1 The fall in the average size of households was partly due to falling birth rates. It was also partly due to young people leaving home earlier to start their own families and to set up their own homes.

2 The decline in the number of houses in the city centre was due to slum clearance. Between 1951 and 1980, 83 255 houses were demolished in Manchester, and only 59 468 new ones were built in the city (23 344 houses were built by the council on overspill estates outside the city boundaries).

(b) Changes to the rural–urban fringe

Middlesbrough is a town that has been losing population too, but these figures show how the number of households has risen, and is predicted to go on rising.

Middlesbrough's population

Year	1981	1991	2001(est.)	2006(est.)
Population	150 000	144 000	143 000	140 000
Households	54 000	55 600	57 800	58 300

People want more houses. They do not want to live in inner city areas. Therefore a lot of new houses have had to be built on 'greenfield sites' on the edges of urban areas. Most of the land that was built on used to be farmland, although it was not very high quality.

There has also been growth of commuter settlements in areas outside the old towns. Some commuter settlements are in rural villages which have expanded as new estates have been built. Other commuter settlements are in completely new towns.

Issues on the rural-urban fringe

You ought to be aware of the issues involved in settlement on the rural-urban fringe, and in commuter villages beyond the fringe.

There is competition between different groups of people who all want to use land on the edge of urban areas. Should this competition be decided by market forces (who can bid the highest for the land) or by planning processes (who deserves the land most)?

One example of the planning process is the Green Belt policy which makes it very difficult to obtain planning permission to build on protected land around urban areas. However, some people say that this leads to a shortage of houses in urban areas and pushes the prices up.

Another planning solution to the pressure on the rural-urban fringe was the government's decision to refuse planning permission for any new, out-of-town shopping centres. New centres now have to be built on brownfield sites – places which have been built on before – rather than on greenfield sites (see below).

Issues in commuter villages

Country villages are nice places to live. People who live there and commute into town can enjoy a peaceful, rural life. However the growth of commuting causes problems:

- for older inhabitants, who may feel that their village has been changed by the newcomers
- for farm workers and other rural workers who cannot afford the prices that are paid by people from the cities
- on roads, where commuters may cause overuse and jams at rush hours
- in rivers, where all the extra building may increase the speed of run off, leading to increased flood risk, etc.

ocus Points 3 and 4

◆ Give two **push factors** that made people want to leave inner city areas. Give two **pull factors** that attracted them to suburban housing areas.

◆ In 1981 the average number of people in households in Middlesbrough was:
$$\frac{150\ 000}{54\ 000} = 2.8 \text{ people.}$$
In 2006 it is estimated that the average household size will be
$$\frac{140\ 000}{58\ 300} = ? \text{ people.}$$

Exam practice

(a) Name an industrial town or city in the UK that you have studied.

   (i) Name an industry which was found in that town in the nineteenth century.   (1 mark)

   (ii) Give one reason why your chosen town was well suited for that industry to develop.   (2 marks)

   (iii) Where did housing develop for the people who worked in your chosen industry? (2 marks)

   (iv) Describe the appearance of the houses in that area, and describe the area's street pattern.   (4 marks)

(b) Many old areas of workers' housing have been redeveloped since the 1960s. Name an area of redevelopment in your chosen town or city and:

   (i) explain why the area needed to be redeveloped   (4 marks)

   (ii) describe how the redevelopment has altered the area.   (4 marks)

(c) With reference to one or more examples you have studied, explain why commuter villages have grown up around the edges of many towns and cities in the UK.   (3 marks)

Out-of-town shopping centres v. CBDs

The central business district (CBD)
CBDs in most cities developed around the most accessible place. This was usually where several roads met, and near to railway and bus stations. When cities first started to grow there was usually a market place near the centre. The market place may still be there, but now most CBDs are dominated by offices and large shops.

- CBDs are very busy areas. This is because people can get to them easily from all directions.

- Because CBDs are accessible there are lots of customers for businesses located there.

- This makes businesses in this area very profitable so many firms want to locate in the CBD.

- Rents in CBDs are usually higher than in other parts of cities.

- All the businesses attract more and more customers to the CBD ... until the CBD is so congested that business starts to decline.

Out-of-town shopping centres
The growth of out-of-town shopping centres has been very important during the last twenty years. They include the White Rose Centre (Leeds), Meadowhall (Sheffield), Merry Hill Centre (Dudley), Lakeside (next to the Dartford Crossing), and many others. What are the advantages of these centres that have led to their rapid growth?

- Land is cheaper on the edge of cities than in the CBDs.

- There is plenty of space for car parking. Stores that need a very large floor area have enough space to build on one level.

- New buildings can be put up without the costs of demolishing old ones, or fitting them around existing buildings.

- They are easily accessible by road, often being close to ring roads, by-passes and motorway interchanges.

Hints and Tips!

In examinations you should usually avoid abbreviations, but 'CBD' is so common that it is safe to use it in geography.

 **ocus Point 5**

Cover up this page and explain why rents of shops in CBDs are usually high.

The growth of out of town shopping produced a lot of competition for CBDs. In order to attract customers, many new developments were introduced into CBDs. These included:

- pedestrian streets, to make shopping pleasanter and safer

- pick-up points where shoppers can bring their cars close to the stores

- covered arcades and malls, to protect shoppers from the weather.

The development of out-of-town shopping centres would not have been possible without mass ownership of cars.

However, by about 1995, the out-of-town centres were falling out of favour with some people and organisations. What were the reasons for this change?

- Growth of new centres used up a lot of the countryside, threatening areas of green belt.

- Shops in city centres were threatened by the competition from out-of-town centres.

- New centres were only really accessible by car. This made it difficult for people without cars (the young, old, disabled, poor, single-parent families, etc.) to use them.

- Increased use of cars causes extra congestion, pollution, etc.

As a result, politicians and planners have brought in stricter rules to make it more difficult to develop out-of-town shopping centres.

Hints and Tips!

Make a table with two headings 'Advantages...' and 'Disadvantages... of out-of-town shopping centres'. Complete the table by writing key words or short phrases in each column. This may be easier for you to learn than the full sentences used here.

Questions

1 Name an example of an out-of-town shopping centre that you have studied.

2 Draw a sketch map to show its location.

3 Label the sketch map to show why this was a good place to build.

4 Describe the market area of the centre. Either do this in words, or draw a map to show the area served by the development.

5 Has the growth of this centre affected trade in the CBD of the local town? If so, how?

Hints and Tips!

In your exam you will be expected to show that you understand how people's different values and attitudes affect geographical decisions. This is a good topic for you to show that understanding. Be ready to explain why some groups can benefit from new, out-of-town shopping centres but other groups cannot use them easily.

Focus Point 6

Cover the page and write down four advantages of out-of-town shopping centres.

The growth of traffic in towns

All towns in the UK have had to struggle to cope with the increased use of cars and lorries in the last few decades. This has been due to:

- increased car ownership, leading to:
  - more use of cars for shopping, and the growth of out-of-town shopping
  - more use of cars for leisure
  - more commuting
  - decentralisation of work from the inner cities to the rural-urban fringe
  - worries about safety, so more use of cars to take children to school

- increased use of lorries because:
  - they allow more flexible transport than railways and canals
  - they are quicker than railways
  - they are essential to service industries in out-of-town sites
  - they are essential for new industrial production methods, like just-in-time (JIT) deliveries.

Car owners and drivers tend to be middle aged, middle class, white, able bodied and male. When towns grow to favour car users, they discriminate against the young, the old, the poor, females, the disabled and ethnic minorities.

Problems of traffic in towns

As well as benefits, cars have caused many problems. For instance they lead to:

- many deaths and injuries to people and wildlife

- air pollution that can cause
  - asthma and other lung diseases
  - acid rain, from the release of sulphur dioxide from exhausts
  - the greenhouse effect, from the release of carbon dioxide

- stress due to noise which constantly affects some people living close to main roads

- more and more space in cities and on the rural-urban fringe being taken up for roads

- damage to buildings by pollution and vibration caused by traffic

- communities being cut in two when major roads are built through suburbs.

Attempts to reduce problems of cars in towns

- One bus can carry as many people as 20 cars, so use of buses cuts down congestion and pollution. Many councils try to encourage the use of buses by park-and-ride schemes, bus priority lanes, increasing the price of car parking, subsidising bus routes, etc.

- Commuter railway systems and tramways have been re-introduced in many cities, although the capital costs of building them are high (e.g. Tyneside Metro, Sheffield Supertram).

- Pedestrian precincts have been developed to try to separate pedestrians from traffic in CBDs.

- By-passes try to separate through traffic from local traffic.

- Urban clearways have been set up to try to stop main routes being blocked by parked cars, etc.

- Traffic calming and lower speed limits have been introduced to try to make residential areas safer.

- Traffic charging is being considered to try to keep non-essential vehicles out of central areas.

Cambridge City Council is considering plans to keep cars out of the city centre. Plans have also been made which will lead to charges for motorists who enter Central London.

Questions

1   Name a town where you have studied the problems of traffic.

2   Describe the problems and say where they are found.

3   Describe some of the attempts that have been made to tackle the town's transport problems.

Exam practice

(a) Imagine that you are a salesperson who works for a soft drinks company. You visit schools in an area that stretches about 50 miles around your office to sell them supplies for their drinks vending machines. Your boss thinks you should use public transport – buses and trains – to do your travelling. Explain why a car would be more efficient and more convenient.   (4 marks)

(b) Road transport damages the environment. Describe two different types of environmental damage caused by:

   (i)   building roads
   (ii) increasing traffic on roads.   (4 marks)

(c) Some towns and cities have problems of traffic congestion in central areas. Choose a town or city where planners are attempting to reduce the problems of traffic congestion.

   (i)   Describe one or more schemes that they have introduced, or are planning to introduce.
   (ii) Explain how the scheme will reduce the problem of traffic congestion.   (7 marks)

The European Union

7 Rich and poor regions in the European Union

At the time that this book was written, in 2002, there were 15 countries in the European Union (EU). At some time in the next few years, up to 10 more countries may join. When they do the EU will change enormously.

The EU was founded in 1956 with the Treaty of Rome. The countries which joined then, and since, have all agreed to bring their economies closer together. They cut customs duties between member states. Then they made their laws to do with the economy more and more standard across the member states. They made it easier for citizens to travel between countries for work, education and leisure. Finally, in 2002, most of the EU members brought in the common currency – the euro.

Regional differences in the EU

The EU is part of the More Economically Developed World. However, there are still big differences in wealth between the richest parts of the EU and the poorest parts.

The map below shows areas with average levels of wealth 20 per cent or more above average for the EU, and areas with levels 20 per cent or more below average.

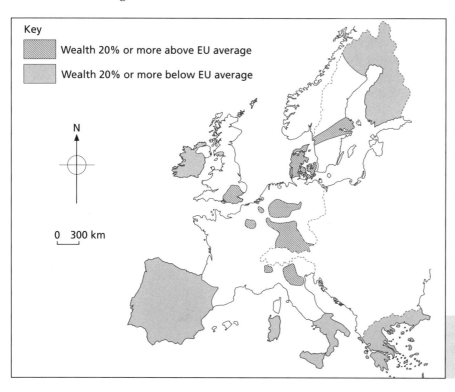

Key

Wealth 20% or more above EU average

Wealth 20% or more below EU average

N

0   300 km

◀ Figure 7.1 Areas of wealth in the European Union

There is one very striking fact about the distribution of rich and poor regions within the EU.

- The richest regions tend to be at the core of Europe.

- The poorest regions tend to be round the periphery.

Some people say that there is a 'hot banana' at the core of Europe. This phrase is useful, because it is easy to remember, but be careful! It is a bit of an over-simplification.

The core area contains:

- most of the major cities

- most of the major ports

- much of the population.

Therefore it has attracted:

- most of the industry

- most of the offices, banks, government, shops, etc.

- many new roads, telecommunications and much technology.

So it can afford better hospitals, education and other services, and attracts more people in an upward spiral of development.

The peripheral area:

- has a difficult climate

- is isolated

- has many areas of poor soils.

Therefore it does not attract much investment and has not developed much industry. Its infrastructure and services tend to be poorly developed. As a result, many of its most dynamic people leave and move to the core, where there are more opportunities.
Many parts of the periphery are in a downward spiral of decline.

How does the EU try to reduce differences between the core and the periphery?
The EU Commission realises that economic development and the integration of the different parts of Europe will not work unless much effort and money is put into developing the peripheral regions. There are three main ways of trying to make this happen.
1 **The Common Agricultural Policy** (CAP) pays subsidies to farmers to help them to modernise their farms.
2 **The European Investment Bank** provides loans for projects to stimulate the economies of underdeveloped regions. It mainly supports large-scale projects, such as steel works.
3 **Structural Funds** are used to help modernisation in regions with out-dated economies. These are usually small-scale projects. The Integrated Mediterranean Programme (IMP) is one example of use of the Structural Fund.

Note If new countries in southern and eastern Europe join the EU they are likely to be poor. This means that they will need a lot of money from the Structural Fund, so there will be less money available for southern Italy and Spain.

8 Farming in southern Italy: problems and development in the periphery

For this topic you should study:
- traditional methods of agriculture
- push and pull factors causing migration from the region
- the effect of migration on the region
- the Cassa per il Mezzogiorno and the Integrated Mediterranean Programme
- the influence of environmental factors (relief, climate, soils)
- land reform and infrastructure changes and their effect on farming.

Italy is a long, narrow peninsula which sticks out into the Mediterranean Sea. Physically there are four main regions:

- the Alps in the North

- the Piedmont, a flat, fertile, alluvial plain to the south of the Alps

- the Apennines, a range of young volcanic mountains

- the coastal plain.

The word **peninsula** comes from two Latin words. *Insula* means 'island'. When '*pen*' is put in front of a word it means 'almost'. So a peninsula is a piece of land with sea on three sides of it. In other words, it is 'almost an island'.

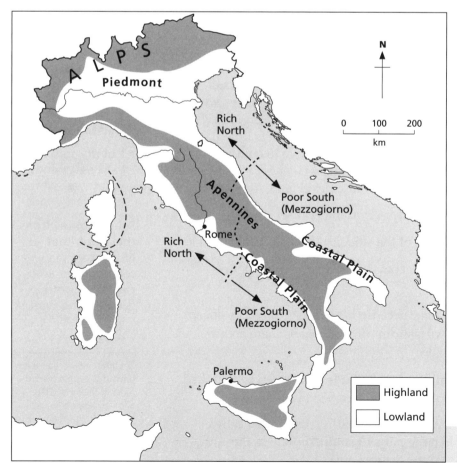

◀ *Figure 8.1 Regions of Italy*

Economically there are two main regions:

- the North, which is rich and developed and part of the European core

- the South or Mezzogiorno, which is poor and far less developed and is on the European periphery.

Physical conditions for farming in the South

The climate of the Mezzogiorno is typical of the Mediterranean climate region (see 'Mediterranean climate' in chapter 9).

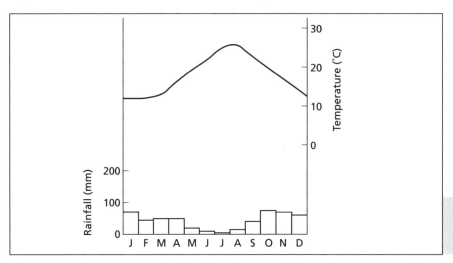

◀ Figure 8.2 Climate of Palermo (see map page 63)

The relief is very broken. Some of the mountains in the main fold ranges rise to almost 3000 metres. The volcano, Mt Etna, is the highest point in the South and is (at present!) 3340m high.

Most of the land is between 200 and 1500m high, with many small ranges of hills. These are separated by deep, steep-sided valleys with fast-flowing streams eroding rapidly into the newly uplifted land. The flood plains of these rivers are rarely very large, so there is little flat land for building or agriculture. Instead, farmers have to cultivate the steep slopes and the hill tops. In many areas they have cut terraces into the hillsides to try and increase the amount of level land.

On the steep slopes soils are usually very thin because:

- water runs off easily, because of the slope, and erodes the soil

- in summer most rain that falls comes in torrential downpours, encouraging fast run-off

- vegetation cover is often poor because it has been grazed by sheep and goats. This also allows fast run-off, and means there are few roots to hold the soil in place

- shortage of flat land means that land that is quite steep is ploughed. This can loosen soil and allow it to be washed away easily.

In these difficult conditions an almost **feudal**[1] system (often called *latifundia*) was still found in large parts of southern Italy at the end of the war in 1945. There were three distinct areas.

ocus
Point 1

The Mediterranean climate has:

- Hot dry summers with east winds
- Warm wet winters with west winds.

Select figures from the graph that illustrate temperature and rainfall in both summer and winter.

[1]'Feudal' means that a few powerful people owned most of the land. They allowed tenants to use some of it, but the poor farmers had very few rights on the land they farmed.

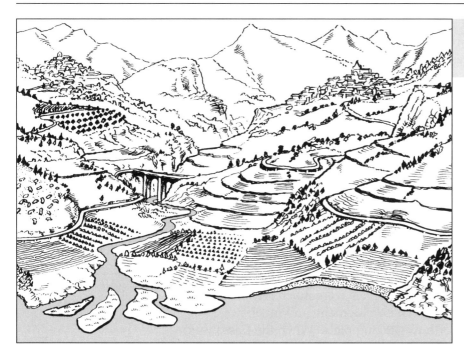

◀ *Figure 8.3*
The landscape of
southern Italy

ocus
Point 2

Cover the page.
Give two reasons to
explain why there is
so little flat
farmland in
southern Italy.

Give three reasons
why the soils are so
thin.

On the coastal plain, where the land is flatter and soils are better, there were some large estates. Parts of these estates were used for growing grapes, olives, citrus fruits and tobacco for commercial purposes. Other areas were rented to peasant farmers to grow subsistence crops of wheat and fruit, and to keep some animals, especially sheep and goats.

Many of the landlords lived away from the area, in the cities, and paid very little attention to their land. Little money was invested in most of the estates so farming methods were backward. It was difficult to sell any surplus crops because of the distance to the big markets in northern Italy. Roads between the North and the South were poor.

Inland, most of the higher, steeper land was rented to peasants for subsistence farming. They grew wheat on patches of flat land scattered around the area, often at a distance of several kilometres from the villages. Vegetables were grown on small plots near the villages. Each family usually owned one or two olive trees and a small area of vines, and had a few sheep or goats which grazed on the poorest land.

In the highest mountains the land was mainly used for grazing sheep and goats, which destroyed much of the vegetation.

Migration from southern to northern Italy

	Birth rate ‰	Income/head (Italy = 100)	Unemployment %	Net migration/year	
				1980s	1990s
Six northern regions (ave)	8.4	117	7.8	+0.3	+4.6
Five southern regions (ave)	12.2	73	18.8	−1.3	+1.4

The table shows some socio-economic indicators and compares the south of Italy with the north. Note that, in the 1980s, Italy was losing population, mainly as a result of emigration to northern Europe. In the 1990s, by contrast, Italy was gaining population, largely as a result of immigration from poorer areas in south-eastern Europe.

Work out some of the pushes and pulls leading to migration from south to north. They can be worked out from your reading of the section on physical conditions and farming in the South.

Pulls to the North included jobs, especially in the factories of the Milan/Turin/Genoa region, a less traditional way of life that appealed to young people, better opportunities for education, and so on.

The Cassa per il Mezzogiorno

In 1950 the Cassa was set up to improve conditions in the South. The area was poor and backward. Income levels were much lower than in the North; there was little industrial employment; and much emigration from south to north was taking place. When the Cassa was set up the Italian government provided £600 million for development work, and the World Bank gave £250 million. In the first ten years the Cassa spent its funds as follows.

56% went on farming improvements
- The Cassa took over land from the big absentee landlords and broke it up into small plots which were given to families to farm. They received enough land to be self-sufficient:
  - 5 hectares if the land was good and could be irrigated
  - more than 5 hectares if it could not be irrigated
  - less than 5 hectares if they already had some land, or another job.

- Small farmers were given cheap loans for farm improvements.

- Agricultural colleges were set up to improve skills.

- Reforestation schemes and river control schemes were introduced to slow down soil erosion and stop flooding.

20% went on infrastructure particularly:
- roads linking rural areas to towns, and the South to the North

- water supply, for domestic use and to improve irrigation

- electricity supply, which also helped the farmers.

24% went on industrial development, education, health care, etc.
By 1960 the investment had improved agriculture, but people were still leaving the South in large numbers. Unemployment was still high. Since then the Cassa has invested in trying to develop industry and tourism to:

- increase employment opportunities

- increase the local market for agricultural produce.

Much of the money for development in the region now comes from the

> **Note** Because the farmers did not own their own land it was not worth them investing in improvements to the land – they could be forced off the land if their landlord wished. The lack of education also meant that the farmers tended to keep to the traditional ways of farming.

ocus
Point 3

Cover the page. Up to 1960, how did the Cassa spend its money? List:
- three ways it invested in agriculture
- three ways it invested in infrastructure
- three other developments it invested in.
Why does the Cassa mainly invest in industry now?

European Union. The **Integrated Mediterranean Programme (IMP)** tries to modernise farming throughout the southern part of the EU.

40% of the budget goes directly to farming to:
- improve the quality of olive and vine growing
- improve animal care, especially through better veterinary care
- improve marketing organisations.

33% of the budget goes to creating off-farm jobs such as craft activities, small-scale industry, small hotels, campsites, etc.

27% of the budget goes to:
- improving fishing by modernising ports and buying new boats
- extending forestry and reducing soil erosion
- education and training.

Unfortunately the amount of money for the IMP is small when compared with the size of the Common Agricultural Policy (CAP). The CAP pays subsidies to farmers based on the quantity they produce. It does not encourage them to grow high-quality produce needed by the market. This means there is still far too much land growing low-quality crops of tobacco, olives, wine and wheat. These are not needed but are bought by the CAP, and kept in store.

Unless the CAP is modernised soon it will go on supporting poor, old-fashioned farming. In addition, the complex structure of subsidies means that illegal organisations can cheat the system. This means that illegal organisations such as the Mafia are still strong, and this all acts to discourage modernisation.

> ### Hints and Tips!
> Make sure you can remember the names 'Cassa' and 'Integrated Mediterranean Programme' (or at least remember IMP).

ocus Point 4

The IMP invests in:
- improving farming
- off-farm jobs
- other projects.

List three ways money is spent on each of these programmes.

Exam practice

(a) (i) On an outline map of Italy, mark the boundary of the Mezzogiorno region. (1 mark)

 (ii) Write a brief description of the climate of southern Italy. Refer to temperature and rainfall conditions in summer and winter. (4 marks)

 (iii) Why does the relief of southern Italy often make farming difficult? (3 marks)

 (iv) Many farmers in southern Italy are 'largely subsistence farmers'. What does this phrase mean? (1 mark)

 (v) Why is access to the market a problem for many farmers in southern Italy? (2 marks)

(b) (i) What is the Cassa per il Mezzogiorno? (1 mark)

 (ii) Describe one of its policies. (2 marks)

 (iii) What is the Integrated Mediterranean Programme (IMP)? (1 mark)

 (iv) Describe one of its policies. (2 marks)

(c) To what extent have the Cassa per il Mezzogiorno and the IMP been successful in raising the standard of living in southern Italy? (3 marks)

9 Tourism in Mediterranean Spain

For this topic you should study:
- location of major tourist areas and reasons for their growth, including a study of the Mediterranean climate
- holiday patterns within Europe (i.e. the origins of tourists to Spain)
- economic importance of tourism
- advantages and disadvantages of tourism to the local economy and environment.

Development of tourism

For many British people Spain **is** the country of holidays. It is associated with 'sun, sea, sand and sangria'. This has come about since the early 1960s due to a combination of factors.

Climate
The two graphs show the temperature and rainfall for Falmouth in south-west Cornwall and Cartagena in south-east Spain. Both places have beautiful scenery, sandy beaches, and many other attractions for holidaymakers, but Spanish resorts have the great advantage of being able to rely on the hot, dry Mediterranean climate in summer.

In summer the area is dominated by high pressure air masses and winds from the east. The air is dry and stable. It brings long periods of cloudless skies, allowing the sun to shine without interruption. This can cause occasional short downpours of convective rain – but these are soon over and rainfall totals are low.

In winter the winds blow in from the Atlantic bringing rainfall, but temperatures stay milder than Britain's, because Spain is further south.

ocus Point 1

Use the graphs to complete the table.

	Cartagena	Falmouth
Average July temperature (°C)		
Average August temperature (°C)		
Average July rainfall total (mm)		
Average August rainfall total (mm)		

What does your table suggest about the number of hours of sunshine and cloud in the two resorts?

What does it suggest about sea temperatures in the two resorts?

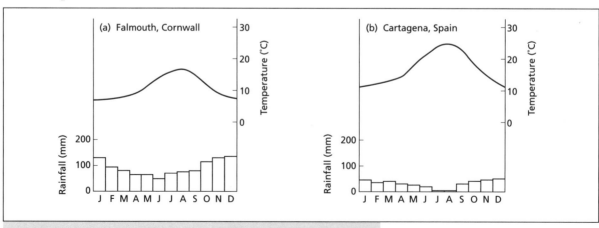

▲ *Figure 9.1 Climate graphs for (a) Falmouth and (b) Cartagena*

Physical environment

Mainland Spain has over 1000km of coastline on the Mediterranean. In addition the Balearic Islands lie just off the coast. Huge stretches of the coast have sandy beaches, and there are also many attractive, rocky headlands which add to the appeal.

The clear blue skies and clean water combine to make the sea look blue. The low tidal range, the lack of strong currents, and gently sloping sand combine to make the sea safe for bathing in most areas. Just inland there are many areas of attractive scenery which can easily be visited, while on the coast itself there are pretty fishing villages and some beautiful, historic cities and ports like Barcelona and Valencia.

Low wage rates

Average wage rates in Spain have been lower than those in northern Europe throughout the period of the growth of the holiday industry. Since Spain joined the EU in 1986 wages have risen but they are still quite low, so prices in hotels, restaurants, etc. are cheaper than in the UK. This increases Spain's attraction.

Cheap air fares

Mass tourism only really became possible in the 1960s with the development of wide-bodied aircraft, especially the jumbo jet. This meant that people could be moved long distances fairly cheaply. Companies that bought these aircraft had to keep them full and flying by attracting new customers. They created the package-holiday industry, which only makes small profits on each person moved, but attracts huge numbers of people to travel.

Building the resorts

Up until the late 1950s, Spain's tourist industry had been very small. The only foreign tourists who visited the country were 'independent travellers' who had enough time, money and initiative to organise their own travel and to discover interesting little places to stay. These were often small, unspoilt fishing villages, with beautiful beaches that had not been discovered by mass tourism.

Then, over a period of about ten years, the situation changed completely. Businessmen realised what natural advantages the Spanish coast offered – if only facilities could be provided for the mass tourist industry, which would bring people in on cheap flights. This meant investing first in hotels and airports, allowing the area to cater for large numbers. As long as the hotels could be filled they could offer very cheap prices. Once the tourists started coming, the villages became towns, with large hotels, restaurants, clubs, shops, pools and other facilities for tourists.

The boom brought rapid development and improvements in wage rates for many people. The infrastructure of roads, water supply, airports, etc. has also been improved, bringing many benefits to local people.

Development has also caused problems. In many places it has damaged the environment: the scenery has been altered, and often spoilt; water has been polluted; traditional industries such as fishing have been

Focus
Point 2

Look back through this section of text.

List five of the Spanish coast's physical attractions for tourists.

Companies could only make a profit if they could sell **all** the seats on their planes. This meant that they had to market their holidays with a very heavy programme of advertising. Price cutting, to attract customers from opposing firms, became very common.

Note Remember, jobs in tourism are usually only seasonal. They cannot be relied on to offer a wage all year round.

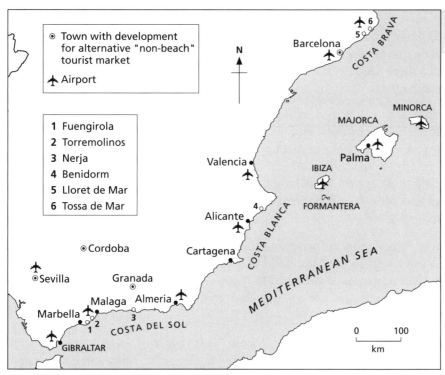

◀ *Figure 9.2 The Spanish tourist industry*

Majorca shows how resorts specialised in different types of holiday. Resorts around Palma in the south of the island specialised in cheap holidays. Large hotels were built to cater for the 'mass market'. In the north of the island resorts were kept smaller to attract people who wanted a quieter holiday in a more traditional Spanish environment. The smaller numbers of people who came to this area were usually able to pay higher prices than the people staying round Palma.

damaged; and so on. All this has been done to develop tourism, and tourism is a very fickle business. Fashions change, and old resorts can be abandoned when the market for holidays change.

Many tourist resorts go through stages of development, then decline.

• **Stage 1** Pioneer development	Single tourists come to explore. There are few facilities. Access is difficult. Local culture is one of the main attractions. The resort becomes fashionable with 'trend-setters'.	
• **Stage 2** Rapid growth	Facilities are developed. Access becomes easier. Mass tourism starts because of better marketing. Tourism starts to dominate the local economy and culture.	
• **Stage 3** Saturation stage	There are so many tourists that the area becomes overcrowded. The original attractions of the area start to be spoilt by overuse. Pollution becomes a serious problem and the resort becomes unfashionable. Growth slows down.	
• **Stage 4** Decline	The market moves on, because the attractions of the area have disappeared. The resort has to seek new gimmicks to attract visitors, or seek new markets.	

The following history 'time line' shows how Spain has gone through some of those stages.

1960	Fewer than half a million British visitors.
1971	More than 3 million British visitors.
1988	Over 7.5 million British visitors. Total of 54 million visitors, mainly from northern Europe. Tourism now accounts for 10% of Spain's GNP.

ocus Point 3

Try to work out when the Spanish coastal resorts were in Stages 1, 2 and 3. Do you think they have reached Stage 4 yet?

1989	Total number of visitors fell by 0.2%. Number of British visitors fell by 4%.
1990	Poor exchange rate makes Spain a poor bargain for foreign visitors. Tourist revenue falls by 22.5%
	10 000 East Europeans invited to Spain for free holidays in an attempt to open up a new area of the market wanting cheap holidays.
	Balearic Islands local government invests £65 million in improving infrastructure and environment.
	Marketing campaign increases number of Japanese visitors by a third.
1990–95	Benidorm invests £317 million in new golf courses, parks and clean-up campaigns to protect environment and attract new visitors.
1990–98	Spanish government invests £50 million in chain of luxury 'Parador' hotels in inland Spain, to attract a new, richer type of tourist. Most of these Paradors are in historic, inland cities.
	Marketing campaign for 'Green Spain' to attract tourists to new, unspoilt areas.
1996	Plans to build the Costa Doñana resort cancelled partly because of worries over its effect on the environment, and partly because it was seen as unnecessary and would damage other resorts' business.

Hints and Tips!

Learn this brief summary of Mediterranean climate first:

Hot dry summers, warm wet winters.

Then use this chapter's text to fill in some of the details.

The best answers in exams also use some precise statistics, so try to learn some from your table summarising Cartagena's climate.

Questions

Choose a holiday resort that you have studied.

1　Learn where it is located on the map of Spain.

2　Describe the natural and 'built' attractions of your resort.

3　Describe how the resort has brought advantages and disadvantages to the local people and economy.

4　Describe how the growth of the resort has affected the environment of the area.

Exam practice

(a) Imagine that you are writing an introduction to a travel company's brochure for holidays on the Mediterranean coast of Spain.
　(i)　Write a paragraph to describe the attractions of the climate.　(4 marks)
　(ii)　Write another paragraph to describe the scenery and other **natural** attractions of the area for holidaymakers.　(4 marks)

(b) (i)　On an outline map of Spain, mark and name a chosen holiday resort.　(1 mark)
　(ii)　Name the region where it is located.　(1 mark)
　(iii)　Describe the accommodation and other facilities that have been built for tourists in your chosen resort.　(4 marks)

(c) The growth of the tourist industry has brought both advantages and disadvantages to the local people in the Spanish resorts.
　(i)　Explain one way the local people have benefited from the tourist industry.　(2 marks)
　(ii)　Explain one problem that the industry has caused for local people.　(2 marks)

(d) The number of British tourists visiting Spain has fallen in recent years. Describe one way that the industry is trying to deal with the problems caused by this fall.　(2 marks)

10a Development of the European urban core: Rotterdam/Europort

For this topic you should study:
- the site, situation and function of Rotterdam/Europort
- the reasons for the growth of the port and the idea of a hinterland
- a planning issue in the conurbation

Development of Rotterdam up to 1945

The original site of Rotterdam was 16km from the sea on the little River Rotte which was one of the distributaries of the Rhine. Rotterdam was sited where a dam was built across the Rotte to stop sea water flooding inland during storms. A port grew at this point, because boats from the sea could not travel farther inland.

Rotterdam's main growth began in 1870. There were three main reasons for this.

- A treaty was signed to allow all states along the Rhine to trade their goods on the river. This led to much more trade passing to the North Sea through Rotterdam.

- In 1872 the New Waterway was built. This is a major canal that allowed very large ocean-going ships to reach Rotterdam.

- The Ruhr valley was industrialising very rapidly, and Rotterdam handled the Ruhr's trade with the rest of the world.

By the 1930s Rotterdam had become one of the most important ports in the world. This was due to its situation near the mouth of the Rhine, acting as the port which linked the major industrial area of Europe with the North Sea and the Atlantic. Its docks and industry had started to spread westwards, along the New Waterway towards the North Sea. However, the Second World War destroyed large areas of industry, docks and housing, so by the end of 1945 the city needed massive rebuilding.

The new ports built since 1945

Before the war the port was being extended westwards. After the war this new building speeded up.

- **Eemhaven** was completed in 1967. Three dock basins were built into the land alongside the New Waterway. This was then the biggest container terminal in the world. It was built with special cranes for loading, unloading, storing and sorting containers.

- **Botlek** was built in 1957, mainly as a port for oil imports. Industry has developed around the oil terminals here and in Europort.

DID YOU KNOW?

Obviously Rotterdam was named after the 'dam' on the 'Rotte'. Amsterdam has a similar site, which also gave the city its name – after the 'dam' on the 'Amstel'.

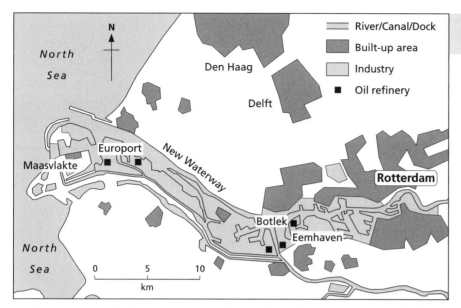

- **Europoort** was built during the 1960s and 70s. A whole series of docks were excavated on the island of Rozenburg. (The earth that was dug out was used to raise the level of the island to 5 metres above sea-level to stop it flooding.) This has more oil tanker terminals and also handles bulk carriers with cargoes of iron ore, other ores, coal and grain.

- **Maasvlakte** is built on land reclaimed from the North Sea (completed in 1974). It has become a port for handling bulk carriers and has a bigger container terminal than Eemhaven. Land is reserved for port facilities. Little industry has developed.

Hints and Tips!

These four Dutch names are difficult to remember. You may find it easier to learn them if you practise saying them out loud. You may be able to remember the sounds better than you can remember the words on the page.

The growth of the oil and petrochemicals industries

Huge supertankers bring crude oil into the docks at Maasvlakte and Europoort. Specialised equipment unloads the oil so quickly that the tanker does not waste time in port. The crude oil is stored in huge, cylindrical storage tanks, grouped together near the terminal in 'tank farms'.

Rotterdam is the biggest oil port in Europe. Many traders meet at the Rotterdam oil market to buy and sell oil. The price everyone in Britain pays for their petrol is largely decided here, and depends on the amount the traders pay to buy their crude oil.

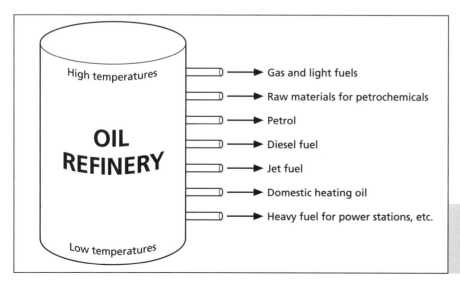

◀ *Figure 10.2 Some of the products of an oil refinery cracking tower*

Most of the crude oil is then sent to one of the five major oil refineries built close to the port. Here the crude oil is broken down into a number of separate substances, by 'cracking' inside a tall, cylindrical structure called a 'cracking tower'.

Some of the products can be used straight away, but others have to be processed further. They are used as the basis for a whole new industry – petrochemicals. The elements in the oil fractions have to be taken apart and put back together again in different combinations in a petrochemical plant. The products made include fertilisers; pesticides; plastics; rubber; paint; dyes; disinfectants; food additives; drugs; etc.

Petrochemical plants consist of complex networks of pipelines, pressurised containers, heating systems, cooling towers, and so on. They are like huge, complicated, magnified versions of some of the experiments that you use in chemistry lessons. They are very capital intensive – which means that a lot of money has to be spent setting up the plant. They are often controlled by computer systems and need only a small workforce of very skilled engineers and technicians.

Distribution of goods to Rotterdam's hinterland

By barge
Most of the bulky goods for distribution to the hinterland are carried along the inland waterways by barge. The Rhine river system allows goods to reach all of the Netherlands, western Germany, Luxembourg, eastern France and northern Switzerland.

This barge system does not just extend along the Rhine. The river system is linked by a series of canals to other parts of Europe.

By rail
The movement of freight by rail has declined enormously over the last 50 years. However, it is still used to move large, heavy loads.

It is also faster than barge transport. There are railway lines running along both sides of the Rhine valley, and trains are sometimes used in preference to the barges when speed is important.

By road
The vast majority of Rotterdam's trade in goods other than bulky raw materials, is carried by road. Most manufactured goods brought to Rotterdam either as imports or exports are carried by road on the overland leg of their journey. Since the integration of European Union economies, the hinterland of Rotterdam has expanded even more. Routes from all of central Europe are linked to Rotterdam. Lorries can move goods to Rotterdam very quickly, and then its position at the southern end of the North Sea allows easy access to the Atlantic.

Rotterdam's hinterland, its trade and its wealth have grown because of:

- its position
- the integration of Europe's economy through the EU
- its excellent road links
- its very modern, efficient port facilities.

In the petrochemical industry the waste products of one plant become the raw materials of the next plant. Petrochemical plants are linked to each other by systems of pipelines. This means that once one chemical works has been set up, it often attracts many others to the same location. This certainly happened around Europort.

'Hinterland' is a German word. Literally it means 'the land behind'. It is used to refer to the area inland from a port that exports and imports goods through that port.

Rotterdam/Europort's functions

In summary, Rotterdam/Europort is one of the world's major ports – especially an oil port. It has a major transport function – including sea, barge, road and rail transport. It is also an oil refining centre and has a wide range of port-based and other industries. There are many administrative, financial and trading jobs linked to the port and its industry.

A planning issue in Rotterdam/Europort

As you have seen, the reason for Rotterdam's existence is its position where one of Europe's major rivers meets the sea. This also presents a major problem to the city authorities. The city can suffer floods from both land and sea.

Floods from the sea

In 1953, gale force winds from the sea, linked to an intense low pressure system, caused a storm surge around the North Sea coasts. The sea swept inland along the Dutch coast, overwhelming the dykes which had been built to protect land that lay close to sea level, or even below sea level in places. Nearly 2000 people died in one night and much of Rotterdam was flooded.

The Dutch solution was the Delta Scheme. This is a series of dykes built around the mouths of the Rhine delta. The dykes are nine metres high – strong enough and high enough to withstand storm surges even bigger than that in 1953. Will that be enough? People now realise that global warming may well cause sea level to rise and bring more stormy weather. The engineers and planners are having to consider whether the Delta Scheme will be enough to protect their country in future.

Floods from the land

In 1995, the lower Rhine valley suffered serious floods. Large areas of land were covered with water and many villages and small towns had to be evacuated. There were even fears that large parts of central Rotterdam could be flooded. Fortunately the levées along the river held and were just high enough to prevent a disaster. However, the disaster had come so close that planners had to consider what had caused the floods to be so severe. They had to ensure that the city would not be inundated next time.

Amongst the many causes of the flood were:

- development of agriculture in the upper basin, which led to faster runoff because trees were removed and soil was drained

- urbanisation of the surface in other parts of the upper basin, again causing faster runoff

- straightening of the river to make navigation easier

- building of levées along the river, which help to contain smaller floods, but which can make big floods more catastrophic

All countries have their own system of road numbering. In the UK motorways are classified as M and the main roads are all A or B roads. The main routes that cross European borders are now classified as E roads.

- protection of some parts of the floodplain upstream which stop floodwater spreading out, and move even more floodwater downstream.

The planners realised that the main problem for Rotterdam was that the water was running down the Rhine too quickly. Something had to be done to slow down the water. They had to store as much water as possible on the flood plain, upstream from the city.

Some of the solutions were:

- to work with EU partners, especially Germany, to encourage forestation and to reduce the speed of runoff in the upper basin

- to allow old river meanders to re-form

- to build wind dykes out into the river to slow down its flow

- to set aside some less valuable areas of the flood plain as storage areas for flood water – moving people who live there if necessary and paying them compensation

- to allow some parts of the flood plain to become wetland nature reserves.

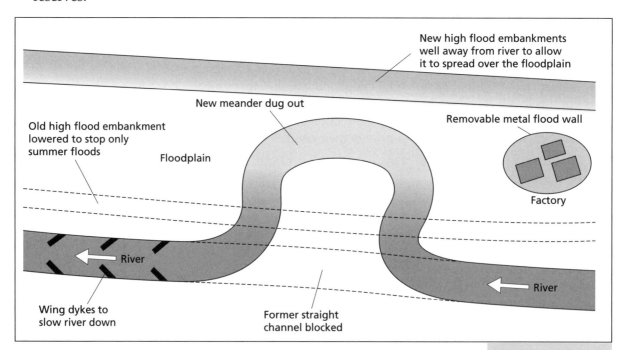

▲ Figure 10.3 Some flood prevention solutions on the River Rhine

In summary, the planners are trying to let the river return to a more natural course. However, they are planning this very carefully to ensure that this valuable resource can still be used for navigation, drainage, water supply and recreation.

10b Development of the European urban core: the Ruhr conurbation

For this topic you should study:
- the site, situation and function of the conurbation
- the reasons for the growth of the conurbation
- a planning issue in the conurbation.

The Ruhr region is one of the biggest conurbations in the world. It became a conurbation during the nineteenth century when several industrial towns grew and merged together. However, several of these towns were first settled in the medieval period. They started as trading towns, thanks to their site on the North German Plain.

The site of Duisburg is particularly interesting. It was built in the medieval period, where two major trade routes crossed:

- the 'Helweg' route from Paris and the North Sea to central and eastern Europe
- the route from Scandinavia and the Baltic to the Mediterranean.

They met at a bridging point over the Rhine. Later on, Duisburg grew because the port on the Rhine was a good place to ship industrial goods from the Ruhr to the rest of Europe and the world.

The growth and decline of heavy industry

The Ruhr industrial conurbation is built on the coalfield which lies beneath the North German Plain, mostly to the east of the River Rhine. In the 1930s this region was described as 'the workshop of Western Europe'. Its main industries were:

- coal mining
- steel making (using the coal and imported iron ore)
- heavy engineering (using local steel and powered by locally mined coal).

The manufacture of chemicals and textiles were also important.

Several medium to large-sized towns developed in the area, and spread to form a conurbation stretching almost 100km from west to east.

Focus Point 1

Copy and complete this flow diagram of heavy industry. Fill in the blanks, using these phrases:

- coal mining
- steel making
- heavy engineering
- imported iron ore.

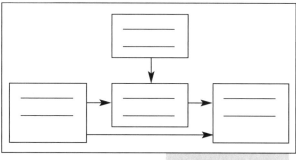

▲ Figure 10.4

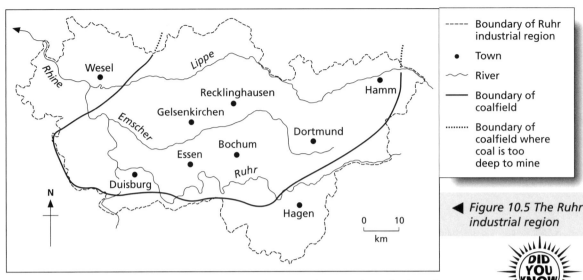

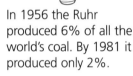

◀ *Figure 10.5 The Ruhr industrial region*

Coal output reached a peak in 1956. Since then production has declined steadily, as shown by the graphs below.

The steel industry has also declined. It reached peak production later than coal mining and its decline has not been as fast as coal's decline. There has been a big improvement in efficiency because production has been concentrated in two very large, mechanised, integrated steel works.

DID YOU KNOW?

In 1956 the Ruhr produced 6% of all the world's coal. By 1981 it produced only 2%.

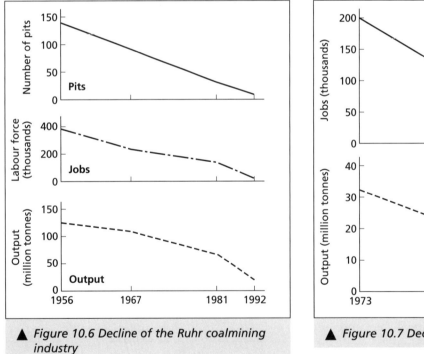

▲ *Figure 10.6 Decline of the Ruhr coalmining industry*

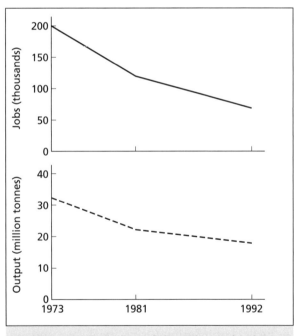

▲ *Figure 10.7 Decline of the Ruhr steel industry*

Changing location of the heavy industry

The cross-section on the next page shows how the coal seams come to the surface in the south of the region, along the Ruhr valley. They dip northwards, becoming deeper and more difficult to reach in the Emscher and Lippe valleys. The earliest mines were in the Ruhr valley where the coal was easy to mine, so naturally the coal in this area was exhausted first.

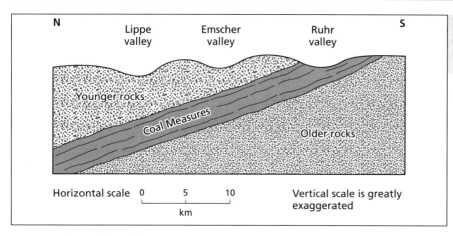

◀ *Figure 10.8a Cross-section through the Ruhr coalfield*

By 1981 the Ruhr valley had no coal mines left. Work was concentrated in fewer, larger, capital-intensive pits further north. Later the pits in the Emscher valley closed and all production is now in the far north of the region. Unfortunately the coal here is very deep and expensive to mine. Although the pits are highly mechanised and efficient, they run at a loss and would close if the government did not pay large subsidies.

In 1981 there were seven integrated steel works in the Ruhr region. These were mainly in the west, close to the Rhine because the iron ore was brought in by barge along the Rhine. There were also four old, small steel works in the Ruhr valley, close to their coal supplies.

Now production has been concentrated at two sites:

- at Hamborn, near Duisburg, on the Rhine, and

- at Dortmund, in the heart of the old coal-mining area, on the Emscher.

British miners are angry that they have to compete against subsidised German coal mines. The UK mining industry has declined far faster than the German industry because of this. (See chapter 4.)

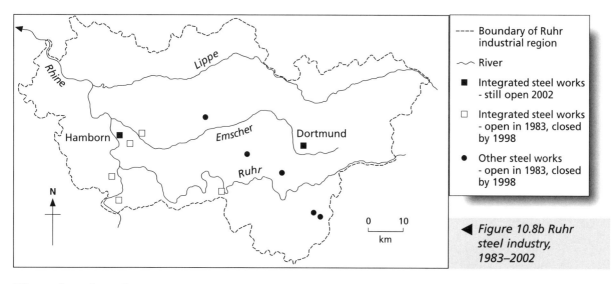

◀ *Figure 10.8b Ruhr steel industry, 1983–2002*

Planning for change

Planning in the Ruhr has two main objectives:
1 To improve the environment which had been scarred by mining and industrial dereliction.
2 To attract new employment to replace jobs lost as heavy industry is closed down.

Planners have been very successful in achieving the first objective. It has been more difficult to achieve the second, because the area still has a poor image, despite the improvements to the environment.

Reclaiming the environment

The Ruhr has had its own regional planning agency, dealing with environmental problems, since 1920. It is called the Siedlungsverband Ruhrkohlenbezirk (SVR). Its aims are:

- to encourage industrial firms to reduce pollution
- to provide and maintain open space on three different scales:
  - small recreation spaces on the edges of urban areas
  - green wedges preserved between the towns
  - large forested parks surrounding the whole conurbation.

Two particular projects are worth mentioning: the Naturpark Hohe Mark, and the reclamation of the Graf Bismarck pit.

The **Naturpark Hohe Mark** covers about 600 km² on the northern edge of the Ruhr region. It consists mainly of coniferous forest. The SVR's task has been to make this area attractive and accessible to the public. A network of footpaths through the forest has been created, with car parks and cafés for walkers. Water sports facilities have been developed in reservoirs on the edge of the park. It is connected to the urban areas by bus and train services to encourage people to use the facilities.

The **Graf Bismarck Pit** was a large, modern mine near Gelsenkirchen, which was closed in 1966. This left 2 600 000 m² of derelict land and waste tips. These have been remodelled to provide:

- dry ski slopes and other recreational activities
- woodland and nature reserves
- tips for waste disposal in areas of subsidence which have now been filled in and grassed over to produce sports pitches, etc.

Hints and Tips!

'Siedlungsverband Ruhrkohlenbezirk' is quite a hard name to remember. If you can learn it you will impress the examiner. If you cannot, make absolutely sure that you remember the initials of the planning authority – SVR. It is much better to know that specific detail, rather than just writing something vague about 'the planners'.

Hints and Tips!

Learn the names of these two schemes very carefully. Do try to get the spellings right. Then learn three features of each scheme.

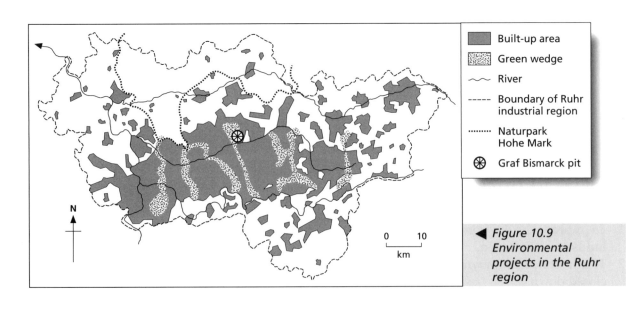

Figure 10.9 Environmental projects in the Ruhr region

The SVR has been so successful that over 60 per cent of the so-called 'industrial area' of the Ruhr is now classified as green open space.

Attracting new employment

Most modern industry is light and 'footloose'. It is not tied to supplies of energy or raw materials like the old heavy industry was. Managers can choose to locate factories:

- near to the market and to cheap labour supplies
- near to highly-trained labour
- in an area with a good infrastructure of roads, airports, etc.
- in areas that have a good environment, leisure facilities or climate.

Since the 1950s the great growth areas of German industry have been in the south of the country, for example in Bavaria and lower Rhine Valley – Munich, Stuttgart and Frankfurt have been particularly successful in attracting new industries. They have certain advantages over the Ruhr region, because they:

- are warmer, especially in summer
- are near attractive mountains such as the Alps and the Black Forest
- do not have an 'image problem' of being linked with heavy industry.

The new industries in these areas include electronics, automobiles, aircraft, light chemicals (especially drugs), optics (lenses, cameras, telescopes, etc.), and especially IT industries.

In order to try and attract such industries and services the Ruhr planners have had to make many changes. The environmental improvements brought about by the SVR are described above. There have been a number of other changes too.

- New motorways now link the centres of the cities of the conurbation (over 500km of new roads have been built in the area since the 1960s).
- Integrated public transport systems, with buses, trains and city centre tram systems, have been developed. Their timetables are co-ordinated to allow fast, efficient travel within and between towns and cities.
- Three new universities have been opened, in Munster, Marburg and Cologne. They teach science-based courses to produce technicians and engineers, and also provide research facilities for industry.

Despite all these efforts, growth of new employment has been slow.

- Essen, which used to be a main centre of the steel industry, has become a centre for modern office-based work. Many small IT firms have been attracted to the town by the banking and insurance offices that have developed there.
- The government has moved civil service jobs to other towns. It has tried to spread the well-paid office jobs to the towns that need new employment.
- Cologne is the centre of Ford's manufacturing in Germany.

ocus Point 2

What are footloose industries?

Give three reasons why they have mainly been attracted to southern Germany rather than to the Ruhr region.

Hints and Tips!

Learn these five headings for the work done by planners to attract industry:

- motorways
- public transport
- universities
- industrial sites
- environment.

When you know the headings, try to learn two or three details under each one. This will allow you to write elaborated answers in the exam.

Unfortunately, unemployment has remained higher in this region than in the rest of western Germany. Since 1965 there has been a steady trickle of migrants out of the Ruhr region. Most of the people leaving have gone to cities in southern Germany where employment is available, and where the environment is more attractive.

Is the Ruhr region an area of poverty?

Three different answers can be given to this question.

1   Compared with other parts of the EU, like southern Italy, the Ruhr is certainly not an area of poverty. Average wage rates are higher and unemployment is lower than in those areas.

2   Compared with the rest of the old West Germany the Ruhr is quite poor. Unemployment rates are higher than in the south, although people with jobs are still well paid.

3   Compared with most of the old East Germany, the Ruhr is not at all poor. It has a much stronger economy than the east, where many areas still rely on old heavy industry like the Ruhr did in the 1950s.

The Ruhr has been through a great transition in the last 50 years. The changes have been managed very carefully. Some people have suffered, but everything that could be done to smooth out the problems has been done. The Ruhr offers many lessons to other old industrial regions about how to plan for the decline of employment in coal and heavy industries. The area's industries have been modernised, and the environment has been restored with great care.

The Ruhr region's functions

In summary, the Ruhr's main functions used to be mining and heavy industry. These have not gone altogether but now the area has a much broader range of functions, including light industry, services, leisure and education. These broadly-based set of functions are largely thanks to careful planning of its industrial change.

Hints and Tips!

The three possible answers to this question depend on scale. The scale of an area is always important to geographers, and you should be prepared to think about different scales when you are answering any geography question.

10c Development of the European urban core: the Paris region

For this topic you should study:
- the site, situation and functions of the conurbation
- reasons for the growth of the conurbation
- a planning issue in the conurbation.

The site and situation of Paris

The city of Paris dates back to the Middle Ages. In fact there was probably a settlement there in Roman and even pre-Roman times.

The original site of Paris was on an island in the Seine, the Île de la Cité. This was chosen because:

- it had a good freshwater supply

- it was easy to defend

- it was a good bridging point over the Seine, because of the island half way across the river.

Unfortunately, as the city grew this good site became a problem. It was very inconvenient to have the city built on both sides of a major river. In the present day this site adds to Paris's traffic problems – but it does also help to make the city a very attractive place for tourists!

In the Middle Ages Paris became the capital of France. As France grew bigger and more powerful the city became more important too. Its situation allowed this to happen because it was:

- at the centre of the Paris basin, a lowland area of very rich and varied agricultural soils

- situated on the Seine, a major navigable waterway, which was linked by canal to other major waterways, including the Rhine

- at a point where routes met, because of its bridges

- located on routes from the North Sea to the Mediterranean and from the Atlantic coast to central and eastern Europe.

The functions of Paris

This situation, and the fact that Paris was the capital of a strong, centralised country, meant that Paris became a centre for a variety of industries and a focal point for trade, administration, the courts, finance, the church, education, culture and, of course, tourism.

Notre Dame Cathedral is built on the Île de la Cité. As well as being a place of worship, it is a major tourist attraction ... and was where the *Hunchback of Notre Dame* was set!

The growth of the city

In the nineteenth century the centre of Paris, around the Île de la Cité contained many major administrative buildings. This area was designed very carefully to present an image of French power and culture – to show the glory of France to the world. Around this inner zone were several areas of very expensive, exclusive housing – spreading south-westwards from the centre.

The industrial areas and working class housing were kept very separate from this central zone. Industry grew along the Seine and its tributary, the Marne. Housing for the workers in this industry spread in an arc to the north and east of the city.

The map below shows how the city's urban zones developed up to the early twentieth century.

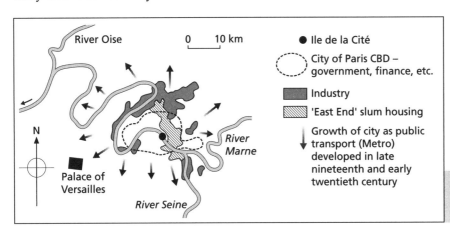

Figure 10.10 Paris in the early twentieth century

Then, during the middle and late twentieth century, the city expanded outwards in all directions.

- Industrial developments took place towards the airports and along the rivers.

- Out-of-town shopping centres grew along the main roads.

- New housing developments took place around the edges of the city.

- New towns were planned and built between 20 and 40 km from the centre.

- Large office developments took place on redeveloped land in the inner suburbs, to try and reduce the over-crowding caused by the concentration of jobs in the city centre.

Disneyland – a special planning problem

In 1985 a site on the edge of Paris was chosen to be the site of Disney's European theme park. This was planned on such a scale that it needed to attract millions of visitors every year if it was to be a financial success. Its site had to be chosen very carefully. It needed:

- a large area of flat, empty land

- an excellent transport infrastructure already in place

Focus Point 2

Here are five fairly brief, general ideas. You need to fill each of these out with one or two examples that you studied in class.

- a large local population, to provide a labour force – and part of the market

- a nearby tourist industry, which could provide hotels etc. for visitors.

Disney's planners chose a site at Marne la Vallee, about 30km to the east of the centre, on the edge of the built-up area.

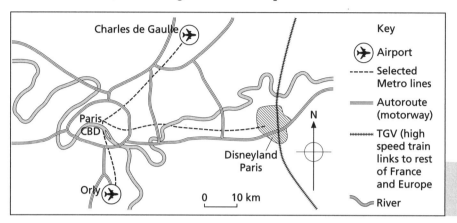

Figure 10.11 The location of Disneyland, Paris

At Marne la Vallee Disney built:

- the theme park with five different 'lands' such as Adventureland and Fantasyland

- hotels, a camp site and self-catering accommodation

- a golf course, ice skating rink and an evening entertainment centre.

They worked with the Paris planners to make sure that:

- the transport system linked directly into the theme park, with a specially-built station and feeder roads to the car parks

- the road system was developed so that congestion was reduced

- the Metro system could carry visitors from the airports, the Eurostar terminal, etc., quickly and conveniently

- the massive demand for water and electricity could be met easily

- the sewage and waste produced by the theme park could be disposed of safely and without causing pollution

- all the extra run-off from the new impermeable surfaces could drain away without causing flooding

- wildlife sanctuaries could be developed around the theme park, to conserve as much wildlife as possible, even though some valuable habitats had been destroyed.

Now, fourteen years after its opening, Disneyland Paris has over eleven million visitors each year and provides employment for over 20 000 people. The careful planning has made sure that the vast majority of these people have enjoyable visits and that they do not disrupt the running of the city.

Hints and Tips!

You might have visited Disneyland in Paris. If so, you could use your experience in an answer on this topic. But plan this carefully! Make sure that what you write is relevant.

10d Development of the European urban core: the Milan/Turin/Genoa industrial triangle

For this topic you should study:
- the site, situation and functions of the conurbation
- reasons for the growth of the conurbation
- a planning issue in the conurbation.

The situation of the conurbation

This conurbation is the centre of industrial and commercial activity in Italy. Turin and Milan both lie on the Lombardy Plain, drained by the River Po. This area has the best farm land in the country but it is also the best place for the location of industry. It has good access to the north and west through Alpine passes, which link the conurbation to the economic core of Europe. It also has access to the eastern Mediterranean through the ports near Venice.

Genoa lies to the south. It is separated from the rest of the industrial area by high land, but the Giovi pass cuts through this high land to give good access to Genoa. As Genoa is on the coast it provides the region's port for trade with the western Mediterranean – and beyond that with the Atlantic, especially with America.

The site of Genoa

It is impossible to study the site of the whole industrial triangle. However, it is easy to describe the site of Genoa. It was built:

- next to a deep-water port

- in a sheltered bay

Hints and Tips!

Try to learn to draw this map quickly and simply. This is a good way to revise and remember facts about the place.

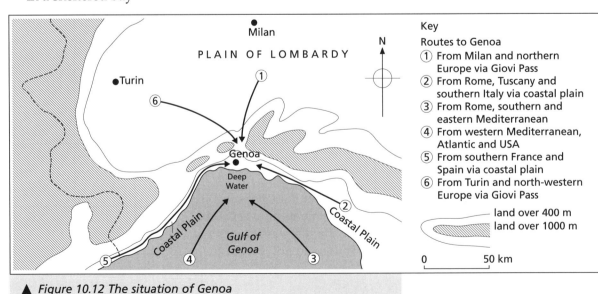

▲ *Figure 10.12 The situation of Genoa*

- at the southern end of the Giovi pass through the Apennines
- on the narrow coastal plain
- on a good route from southern France to Rome and southern Italy.

The growth of the conurbation

As each town became a major economic centre they all grew until they became a major industrial region. This region is not continuously built-up but the three centres are very closely inter-linked, for example:

- Genoa imports raw materials and exports goods for the whole region
- Genoa's steel works produces steel for the Fiat factory in Turin
- the three towns are linked by motorways and express rail routes
- industries and services grew around intersections of these routes
- workers have moved into the area and live in and around the towns
- the concentration of industry and population has brought an increasing demand for services, leading to further growth
- as the main cities have grown, commuters have moved out into small towns and villages in the industrial triangle, causing the rural-urban fringe to become more and more densely populated
- component factories and branch factories of the main companies have also developed in the small towns throughout the area.

Planning issues in the conurbation

The industrial triangle is becoming overcrowded and settlements are sprawling into each other. This is leading to a fall in the quality of life and a reduction in economic efficiency.

The reasons for this include:

- air and water supplies are polluted with waste from the factories and from cars and homes
- congestion on the roads increases journey times and stress
- land prices are rising, and so are house prices
- competition for labour has pushed up wage rates
- people are moving to the area for work, adding to overcrowding
- parks and open space on the rural-urban fringe are being built on.

Some solutions that have been attempted

Local planning solutions

- Strict planning laws now restrict building on greenfield sites.
- Strict pollution control laws have been introduced.

Rich Italians who work in Milan or Turin often buy homes in villages and small towns in the Alps. They commute to work by train and/or car, but can enjoy a lovely living environment, including winter sports opportunities.

• Public transport is being improved to reduce cars on the roads.

National planning solutions

Of all the EU countries Italy is probably the one with the biggest differences between its 'economic core' and its 'economic periphery'. You can find this referred to in chapter 8 which describes the rural south of Italy. Many of the problems of the north are the mirror image of the problems of the south; too much industrial growth as opposed to too little growth, and too much in-migration as opposed to too much out-migration. So, many of the solutions to the problems of the Mezzogiorno were also designed to help the north. For instance:

• investment in large industries – such as the steel works at Taranto – reduced the pressure of too much industry in the north. Also, by keeping workers in the south, it reduced the pressure of migration

• Fiat built a new factory at Melfi in the south. This also reduced pressure in the north, and meant that Fiat could use the cheaper workforce in the south

• all the work of the Cassa per il Mezzogiorno and the Integrated Mediterranean Programme is designed to stimulate the rural and small town economy of the south and lead to more balanced development in the country as a whole.

In addition to this, the Italian government set up some areas which they called 'Third Italy'. Third Italy is an area of medium development which:

• is not as well developed as the industrial triangle but not as poor as the Mezzogiorno

• has wage rates that are lower than in the north but higher than in the south

• has reasonably good access and communications.

The government made it easy to obtain planning permission to set up small factories and other businesses in this area. They also provided financial support for small, specialised firms which set up there.

The biggest success story for this policy has been the development of fashion clothing manufacture in the area around Prato. Milan is the centre of the Italian fashion industry, but the big fashion houses need many small, very adaptable factories to make up small runs of high-quality fashion garments. Speed and skill is essential with these firms. Prato is accessible but much less congested than Milan. Wage rates are also lower, but the workforce is skilled. With government backing it has been the perfect location for the decentralisation of the fashion industry.

▲ Figure 10.13 Economic development in the south of Italy

Have the planning policies been successful?

There have been some successes in the policies to attract new industries to the south and to Third Italy. These are shown on the map (Figure 10.13). The growth of new industry in the Milan/Turin/Genoa triangle has also slowed down. The pollution of air and water is also coming under control – but slowly.

However, the problem of overcrowding remains and is getting worse. The big growth sector in the Italian economy (as in the UK economy) is the service sector. The north is still very attractive for firms in this sector. Financial services and ICT-based companies are growing rapidly. In many ways the attractions of northern Italy are similar to the attractions of England's M4 corridor – and the problems that are being caused by the growth of the service economy are the same in these two areas.

Exam practice

Note Students taking this exam can choose to study any one of four urban core regions. This will make it difficult to set exam questions. They might come in any one of three different forms.

- A question with four completely separate parts, one on each urban region. However, this will take up a lot of space and it will be difficult for students to find their way around. To see what each part of such a question might look like see *GCSE Geography for AQA Specification B* by Helm and Robinson.

- A very general question which says:
  'Choose one urban core region in Europe. For your chosen region:
  (i) describe its site
  (ii) describe its situation
  (iii) explain how its functions have developed….' and so on.
  This makes a rather dull question.

- A question which asks students to apply their understanding to an urban core region which they have not studied. They will be given data about this other region and asked to draw some conclusions from that data, applying their knowledge. Then, at some stage in the question, they will be asked to write something about the region they have studied. The following is an example of such a question.

1 All major cities have planning problems. For instance, in the 1980s, Lille in northern France was a run-down industrial conurbation. The main issue facing planners was 'how do we bring new jobs to Lille?' Fortunately, as the European Union developed, the position of Lille seemed to make it suitable for new developments.
   (a) Study Figure 10.14.
       Explain why Lille's position in the EU made
       it an attractive place for the development
       of new industries and services. (3 marks)

Key

———— Motorway

– – – – – – High speed train line

················ High speed train line under construction

► *Figure 10.14 Lille – transport links*

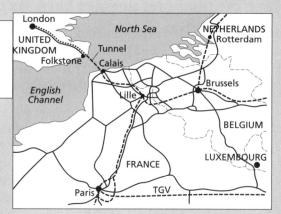

(b) Study Figure 10.15 and Figure 10.16.

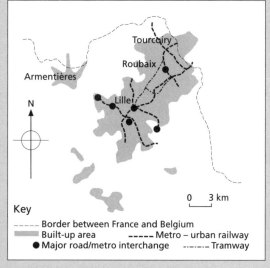

▲ *Figure 10.15 Lille – urban transport systems*

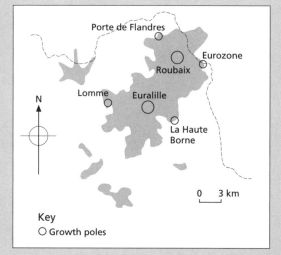

▲ *Figure 10.16 Lille – growth poles (see below)*

Euralille – an international business centre, with an exhibition centre and modern office space

Lomme – built round a transport centre where road, rail and metro meet. Planned to develop processing and export industries, particularly linked to the UK

Porte de Flandres – similar to Lomme, with links to Belgium and Holland

Eurozone – spreads across the border into Belgium; concentrates on financial services

Roubaix – or Euroteleport, will attract call-centres with contacts throughout Europe

La Haute Borne – main high-tech research centre

(b) (i)   How have planners made Lille an easy city for commuters, shoppers etc. to travel in?

   (ii)   Suggest how Lille's planners have tried to attract new employment to the city.

   (iii) Choose one of the growth poles shown. Explain why its location was chosen.

(3 + 2 + 3 marks = 8 marks)

(c) Choose one of the following urban regions which you have studied:

   (i)   Rotterdam/Europort

   (ii)   the Ruhr conurbation

   (iii) the Paris region

   (iv)   the Milan/Turin/Genoa industrial triangle.

For your chosen region describe an issue that presents a problem to planners in that region, and explain what planners have done to deal with that issue.   (9 marks)

11 The links between eastern England and the EU

For this topic you should study:
- one major east coast port, its road links, its port infrastructure and its sea links to Europe
- the Channel Tunnel and its road and rail links.

Everyone knows that a port is a place where ships come in to land and to load and unload. They do not always remember that it is also the place where land transport meets the ships and loads and unloads. The docks are a vital part of the port, but the railway sidings, the lorry parks, the warehouses and so on are equally important. The flow diagram shows the traffic moving one way, but it moves the other way too.

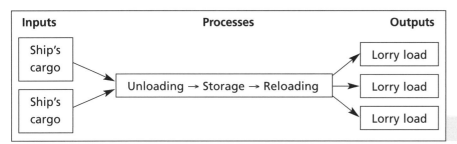

◀ *Figure 11.1*

As cargoes are unloaded, stored and reloaded, it is often convenient to do other work on them too. Loading and unloading adds handling costs, so it is more economic to process raw materials before they are distributed around the country. Therefore industry often develops in ports.

Growth of the east coast ports

In the last few decades, ports in the east and south-east have grown. The reasons are summarised on the map (Figure 11.2) on page 92.

Dover

Dover is a good example of a port that has grown rapidly during the last 40 years. Its growth has been caused by a combination of new technology and changes in the UK's relationship with Europe.

How new technology helped Dover to grow
- Roll on/roll off ('ro-ro') terminals allowed lorries to drive straight on and off ships without needing to load and unload their contents.

- Development of containers and specialised cranes speeded up handling of cargo.

- Newer, larger ferries allowed faster, smoother sea crossings and this attracted more customers.

- Better navigation techniques allowed crossings to continue in almost all weather conditions.

Hints and Tips!

Much of the trade from the east coast ports goes into Europe through Rotterdam. Many of the ideas in this section are very similar to those relating to Rotterdam in chapter 10a. You might revise more efficiently if you study these two chapters together.

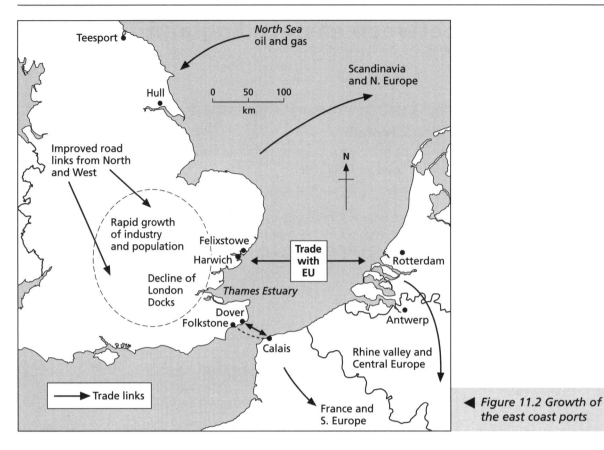

Figure 11.2 Growth of the east coast ports

How changes in the UK's relationship with Europe helped Dover to grow

- Membership of the EU increased the UK's links with Europe.

- Reduction of customs barriers encouraged trade with the EU.

- Closer contacts with EU countries encouraged more visits by holidaymakers, school parties, business people, etc.

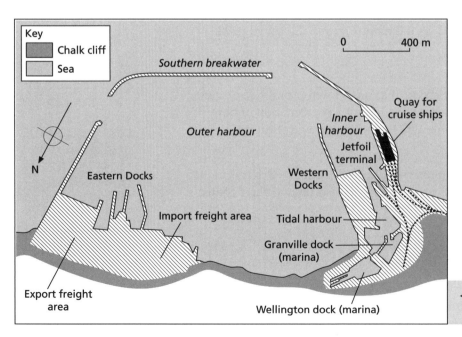

Figure 11.3 Dover docks

Ferry transport

Most of Dover's trade is carried on ro-ro ferries (roll on, roll off). These ferries carry cars, coaches and lorries which can drive on to and off the ships. They do not need any expensive cargo handling equipment.

The ro-ro ferries use the Eastern Docks. The vehicles can drive into the waiting areas straight from link roads to the M2 and M20 motorways. Loading is quick and efficient so that the ferries can make as many trips as possible – and earn maximum profits. Each ferry aims to make 10 crossings per day. Each crossing takes 90 minutes. There are over 100 crossings each day to Calais, as well as crossings to Dunkirk, Ostend and Zeebrugge.

High speed catamarans, or Sea Cats, also sail from Dover. They are also ro-ro, but make the trip in 50 minutes, against 90 minutes for the ships, so they are more expensive.

Container transport

Containers are large steel boxes, built to a standard size. Most of the freight that passes through Dover is in containers. Many of the containers that are imported through Dover are chilled or refrigerated and contain fresh fruit and vegetables. There is a special temperature-controlled warehouse for these.

Special handling facilities have been built for the containers. Cranes on rails can lift the containers on and off lorries or trains and move them to storage yards. Then other cranes lift them on and off ships. To set up this mechanised handling was an expensive investment but it saves money in the long run because it cuts time and costs by:

- speeding up the movement of freight
- cutting the turnaround time for ships
- reducing labour costs
- reducing breakages and theft.

Other port activities

The Western Dock has a marina for pleasure boats. There are also two cruise terminals. Liners stop here on brief visits to south-east England.

The Channel Tunnel

The Tunnel links Folkestone with Calais. This route was chosen because:

- it is the shortest route between England and France
- the rock is chalk marl which is impermeable (keeping the tunnel dry) and soft (keeping building costs low)
- it is well placed for motorway links. The Folkestone terminal lies at an exit point on the M20 and the Calais terminal lies at a node point where motorways to Paris, western France, eastern France, Belgium and the Netherlands all meet.

The main reason for much of this new technology is to reduce the labour force needed to load and unload ships. This reduces costs, which means that prices can be cut and profits increased.

The fire in the Channel Tunnel in 1997 did cause serious disruption to its operations. It also made many people worried about its safety. This helped Dover, because it increased the number of ferry-users, but people soon went back to the Tunnel when they felt reassured that it was safe.

Focus Point 1

Do you think that Dover will continue to grow? Cover up the page, and then give reasons for your answer to this question.

Travel time by the tunnel is only 35 minutes (compared with 90 minutes by ferry). The tunnel is also unaffected by bad weather, unlike the ferries.

Trains, such as Eurostar, can run directly through the tunnel and on to the rail systems of the UK and Europe. People can travel from central London to central Paris in three hours. This is faster than by plane! It has had the effect of 'bringing London and Paris closer together'.

Questions

Choose a port on the east coast of England.

1 Describe the site of its dock area.

2 Describe its situation, or its links with the rest of this country and its trade partners.

3 Explain how its trade has developed over the last 30 years or so, giving clear reasons for the change.

Exam practice

(a) Choose a port on the east or south-east coast of England that has seen an increase in its freight traffic in recent years.

   (i) Mark and name that port on an outline map of the UK.   (1 mark)

   (ii) Explain why its geographical situation has helped to cause the increase in its trade.   (4 marks)

   (iii) How is your chosen port linked to its hinterland?   (1 mark)

   (iv) Describe some of the cargo-handling facilities that have made the port attractive to companies importing and exporting freight.   (4 marks)

(b) (i) Name a port that has an important ferry service for cross-Channel passengers, and cars.   (1 mark)

   (ii) How is the passenger trade of the port likely to be affected by increased use of the Channel Tunnel?   (4 marks)

95

The wider world

12 Amazonia: development in the rainforest environment

For this topic you should study:

- the location of Amazonia
- the equatorial forest environment, with particular reference to:
  - description and simple explanation of the annual distribution of temperature and rainfall, including the causes of convective rainfall
  - relationships between climate, soil and vegetation in the ecosystem
  - traditional subsistence and modern farming systems
- the possibility of sustainable development of the rainforest
- the role of international aid donors in encouraging sustainable development
- eco-tourism and sustainable development

Most of Amazonia consists of the low, flat flood plain drained by the Amazon River and its tributaries. Large parts of the Andes range drain into the Amazon from the west. The older and lower Venezuelan highlands to the north and the Brazilian highlands to the south are also drained by tributaries. The Amazon is the world's second longest river, after the Nile. However, very high rainfall in many parts of the huge basin means that the Amazon has a much bigger volume of water than the Nile.

The Amazon basin contains the largest rainforest on Earth, and large parts of Amazonia are still not fully explored. Much of the forest is still

So much water flows into the Atlantic from the mouth of the Amazon that the water is still fresh enough to drink about 90km from the coast.

◀ *Figure 12.1 Amazonia*

largely unaffected by human activity, but development now threatens many areas of forest. To understand how the rainforest works, and how it can be damaged, it is useful to see the forest as a system, with inputs, processes and outputs.

The tropical rainforest environment – a system model

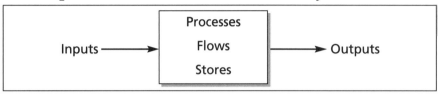

Inputs ⟶ Processes Flows Stores ⟶ Outputs

◀ *Figure 12.2*

The main **inputs** are:

- minerals from soil
- heat + light from the sun (temperature is high all year)
- moisture from rainfall (rain falls all year round)

Plants can grow for 12 months every year.

The main **storages** in the system are:

in the soil
- minerals from weathered rock
- **humus** from decayed plant and animal material
- water

in the vegetation
- minerals and nutrients are used to form plant matter (**biomass**)

on the ground
- dead and decaying plant matter (**litter**)

In the rainforest ecosystem more energy and nutrients are stored in the vegetation than in the soil. This is because the decay of dead matter, and the take-up of nutrients by the plants, is so fast in the hot, humid environment.

Flows constantly transfer matter and energy from soil to vegetation to the litter layer and back into the soil. These flows include:

- the take-up of water and minerals by the plant roots
- dead leaves falling to the ground
- decayed leaf material being carried into the soil by worms.

When rainforest is left in its natural state there are very few **outputs**.

- Water is lost from leaf surfaces by **evapotranspiration**.
- Some water runs into rivers as **throughflow** or **overland flow**.
- Water running through the soil **leaches** some minerals out of the soil.

Because the temperature is high throughout the year, rainfall is heavy in all seasons too. In fact rain falls on 300 days a year or more, in many parts of Amazonia. It has been said that there is more variation in the weather on a single day than there is between the seasons.

The main thing that limits growth of new plants is shortage of sunlight. The thick canopy cuts out about 80% of sunlight and makes the forest floor a very shady place.

Rainforests have very luxuriant vegetation but soils are usually very poor. This is because most of the nutrients are taken up by fast-growing plants.

Focus Point 1

Cover up the page. Explain why rain-forest trees often have tall, straight trunks and a thick canopy of leaves.

Some important **processes**:

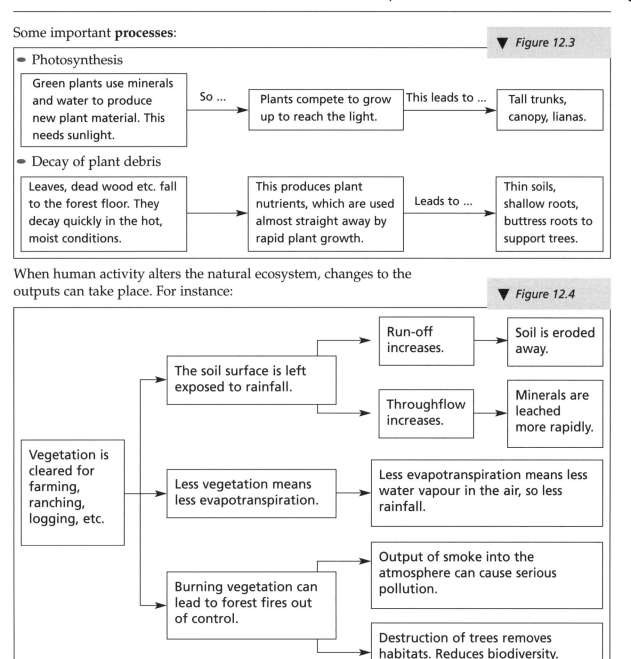

▼ *Figure 12.3*

- Photosynthesis

| Green plants use minerals and water to produce new plant material. This needs sunlight. | So ... | Plants compete to grow up to reach the light. | This leads to ... | Tall trunks, canopy, lianas. |

- Decay of plant debris

| Leaves, dead wood etc. fall to the forest floor. They decay quickly in the hot, moist conditions. | | This produces plant nutrients, which are used almost straight away by rapid plant growth. | Leads to ... | Thin soils, shallow roots, buttress roots to support trees. |

When human activity alters the natural ecosystem, changes to the outputs can take place. For instance:

▼ *Figure 12.4*

Vegetation is cleared for farming, ranching, logging, etc.

- The soil surface is left exposed to rainfall.
  - Run-off increases. → Soil is eroded away.
  - Throughflow increases. → Minerals are leached more rapidly.
- Less vegetation means less evapotranspiration. → Less evapotranspiration means less water vapour in the air, so less rainfall.
- Burning vegetation can lead to forest fires out of control.
  - Output of smoke into the atmosphere can cause serious pollution.
  - Destruction of trees removes habitats. Reduces biodiversity.

Human influences on the rainforest ecosystem

People have always made use of rainforests. They have used the land for farming and mining, they have used the trees for fruit, nuts, medicines, building wood, firewood and even for magic rituals, and they have hunted and domesticated animals and birds. However, in the past forty years or so the rate of use has increased, and the area that is seriously affected has grown rapidly.

Many human activities can be sustainable, if they are well managed; but if they are badly managed they can destroy the ecosystem on which they are based. Some examples are given on page 98.

Sustainable development means:

- encouraging development so that people can have an improved standard of living

- making sure that the environment is not destroyed, so that the improved standard of living will last.

	More sustainable	Less sustainable
Shifting cultivation	Small groups of people use the land to grow crops. Patches of forest are cleared; crops are grown; soil fertility declines; the patch is abandoned and left to recover. The group move on to a new patch of land.	The population of tribes has grown as health care has been improved. Other groups have lost some of their traditional land to outsiders. In both cases they have to use land more intensively. This takes more out of the soil, so it has less time to recover.
Timber	Trees have always been cut by local people to use for building and fuelwood. They took what they needed and left the rest of the forest unchanged. Some commercial timber companies (e.g. in Thailand) replant trees in areas they clear. They plant species that will be useful later. This reduces biodiversity, but does maintain forest cover.	Logging companies use large machines to cut roads through the forest, and then to cut the trees they need. They often clear unwanted trees to allow access to the few valuable trees. Unwanted trees and plants are burnt. This leads to whole areas being cleared of vegetation.
Commercial farming	Plantations for rubber in Malaysia and palms in West Africa have been developed to conserve the soil by making sure that there is always some plant cover to reduce the rate of leaching. They also employ local labour, providing training and good working conditions. This is now being tried in Amazonia, inland from Belém.	In Amazonia large firms clear enormous areas for cattle ranching. Natural vegetation is burnt; grass is planted; cattle graze the area for a few years; then the soil is exhausted and the land is abandoned. The forest does not re-grow as such large areas have been cleared so that seeds can only spread back very slowly. Soil is often very badly eroded.
Mining	Mining can never be truly sustainable. It uses up resources. But in the Carajas region of Brazil the mining company aims to mine iron ore without damaging the forest around the mine. The whole mine area is strictly controlled to stop squatter settlements developing around the mine and the town where workers live.	In Amazonia, mining of iron ore, gold, etc. has caused great damage. Natives have been killed or removed; forest has been totally destroyed, for the mines and for towns, roads and railways. Then large numbers of squatters have moved into the area to make money growing food for the miners, or seeking casual work at the mines. They cause deforestation to spread out from the original mining area.

Farming and its impact on the environment

Deforestation can bring many important changes to the environment. Many of them are damaging, although it is difficult to get precise information about the effects. The effects can be seen at the local, regional and even global scale. Some of them are described below.

Local-scale effects

1 **Soil erosion** – loss of vegetation removes protection for the soil. Leaves intercept rainfall, and roots bind the soil together. When trees are gone, the soil can be washed away easily.

2 **Soil degradation** – low nutrient content of the soil means that when the vegetation is removed, the soil soon loses its fertility. Nutrients are washed out of the soil (leached) and the soil becomes useless.

3　**Sediment in rivers** – is increased, because of the soil erosion. When it is deposited it can block rivers and cause flooding.

Regional-scale effects

1　**Loss of biodiversity** – the rainforest contains many species that are useful, and many more that may be useful in future. Clearing the forest can lead to extinction of both plant and animal species.

2　**Loss of native peoples** – as the environment is altered, some tribes have been wiped out. Others have lost their culture and become absorbed into Brazilian society. New diseases have also been introduced which have caused great suffering to the tribal people.

3　**Change in the water cycle** – some estimates suggest that 50 per cent of all the rain falling on a rainforest is evaporated from the ground and then forms cloud and rain. If the forest is cleared, the rate of run-off increases. This means that less water is evaporated, so rainfall totals over the whole region are reduced.

> *Hints and Tips!*
>
> Learn an example of one area where each type of development is taking place.

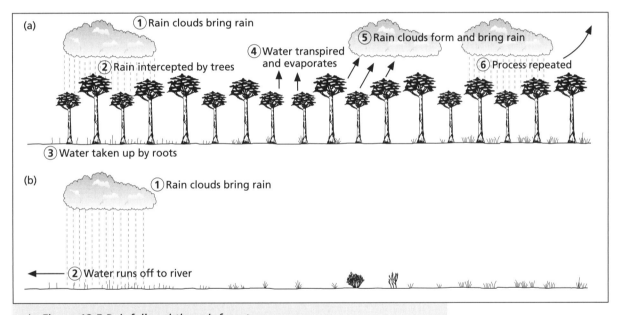

▲ *Figure 12.5 Rainfall and the rainforest*
(a) Water recycled by the rainforest　(b) Water cycle after deforestation

Global effects

Changes to carbon dioxide in the atmosphere – trees contain carbon taken from the air during photosynthesis. When a tree is burnt, the carbon is released into the atmosphere as carbon dioxide. This adds to the greenhouse effect, increasing global warming.

Burning of the rainforest is a less important cause of global warming than the burning of fossil fuels. Some scientists even say it is not a cause of the greenhouse effect, because new plant growth which replaces burnt forest uses up the carbon that was released by the burning.

However, conserving the rainforest is important for many reasons, and citizens of more developed countries should help Brazil to develop their economy without causing further enormous losses of rainforest.

 **ocus Point 2**

Cover up the page. List the effects of deforestation, including:

two local-scale effects

two regional-scale effects

one global effect.

Why is development still taking place?

The development of Amazonia has caused much concern about the environment. Despite the problems, the Brazilian government feels that it is essential to press ahead with development. The country's social problems are so serious that something has to be done to help the poor. Allowing them to settle in the rainforest and farm the land is one of the cheapest ways of giving opportunities to some of those people.

The new settlers cannot concern themselves with long-term conservation – they worry about survival. They exploit their new land, and when the ground loses its fertility they move on and clear more land. Every time this happens, the problems of soil erosion, loss of habitat and loss of species, are increased.

Anyone who is concerned about the problems of deforestation must also consider the problems of Brazil's poor. If they are to be stopped from exploiting the rainforest resources, an alternative must be found. Can an alternative, sustainable development policy stop the damage to Amazonia?

Perhaps concentrating development at growth poles such as Carajas will help to conserve other areas of the rainforest. It may be useful to think of the growth poles as 'honeypots' for development. (See chapter 3, page 30.)

Eco-tourism – a form of sustainable development?

One way that sustainable development is being encouraged is through eco-tourism. This depends on people travelling to areas of unspoilt environment to enjoy seeing them and also to learn about them. The tourists want to develop a greater understanding of the environment, but they also contribute to the conservation of the area they have gone to see. Hopefully, their money helps to make sure that the environment is still there for future generations to enjoy.

At the same time local people are employed in the development and the conservation work, so that they can achieve a higher standard of living but still sustain their traditions. The community can benefit from the visitors, rather than having their way of life overwhelmed and destroyed.

However, there is no opportunity for outsiders to make huge profits – although obviously the travel agents who arrange visits and the companies who provide transport do make reasonable profits. So who provides the capital to set up such eco-tourist developments?

The Cistaline Jungle Lodge, Alta Floresta
This is an eco-tourist project in the heart of Amazonia.

- Alta Floresta is a forest reserve, set up by the Brazilian government.

- It is an internationally famous site for bird species.

▲ *Figure 12.6 The location of Alta Floresta*

- The lodge is a hotel set up with the help of charities, co-ordinated by the Rainforest Action Network.

- The lodge is comfortable but basic and is ecologically sustainable, e.g. waste is composted so that it does not pollute the environment.

- All access is by boat – to reduce pollution and to stop destruction of the forest for roads and airstrips.

- There are opportunities for bird watching, trekking, canoeing, swimming and fishing.

- Local people are trained to work in the lodge, as guides for the tourists and to teach visitors about the ecosystem.

- The local research centre also works with local people to develop sustainable agriculture.

- The research centre is also trying to find resources from the trees and plants in the forest that can be used for medicines, food crops, etc. If they do, the profits from these developments will stay in the local communities.

- Profits from the venture have been used to set up schools, adult education projects and hospitals.

Hints and Tips!

In your examination you may not be able to provide easy answers to the question of an alternative, sustainable development policy, but you must be aware of the issues, and you must be able to consider the point of view of Brazil's landless poor!

Exam practice

(a) In the UK the average monthly temperature is about 17°C in July and about 4°C in January. The seasonal pattern of temperature in Amazonia is very different from this.

   (i) Describe the seasonal pattern of temperature in Amazonia. (2 marks)

   (ii) Explain why Amazonia has very high temperatures. (3 marks)

(b) Many parts of Amazonia have over 2000mm of rainfall per year. Rain falls on more than half the days in the year. Explain what causes this rainfall. You may use a diagram to help your explanation. (4 marks)

(c) (i) In the rainforest vegetation system, what is:
- the canopy
- an emergent
- a buttress root? (3 marks)

   (ii) Choose one of the vegetation features listed in (i). Explain how the climate and soil conditions cause it to develop. (3 marks)

(d) Clearing rainforest causes (i) exposed soil, (ii) reduced evapotranspiration, and (iii) forest fires. Describe how each of these can cause problems for people and the environment. (3 marks)

(e) (i) Why might some people be attracted to go on an eco-tourist trip to Amazonia? (2 marks)

   (ii) How can eco-tourism help local people? (3 marks)

13 The Ganges delta: dense population in a high-risk environment

For this topic you should study:
- the location of the Ganges delta, its formation and physical features
- description of tropical monsoon climate
- the causes and consequences of tropical storms and floods
- effects of monsoon failure and tropical storms
- traditional rice farming
- effects of the introduction of intermediate technology and scientific developments linked with the Green Revolution
- factors affecting birth and death rates in either India or Bangadlesh.

The map below shows the drainage basin of the Ganges river system. To the north lie the Himalayas and to the south is the Deccan Plateau. The river flows into the Bay of Bengal, through its **delta**. Here the river splits up into smaller channels, called **distributaries**.

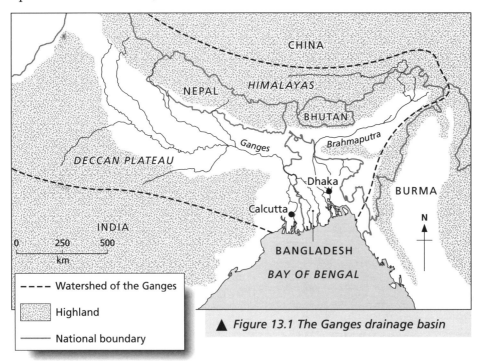

▲ Figure 13.1 The Ganges drainage basin

The Himalayas are recent fold mountains. Many fast-flowing streams carry eroded sediment down from the mountains, and much of this has been deposited to form the flood plain of the Ganges basin.

- This sediment, which is renewed every year by flood water, provides excellent soils for rice cultivation.

- The area's monsoon climate provides ideal rainfall and temperature conditions for rice growing.

The tropical monsoon climate

The Ganges basin lies in the region of monsoon climate. This means that the seasonal pattern of rainfall is very uneven.

There are three main seasons in the Ganges basin (see Figure 13.2).

1 **The hot dry season**   The sun is overhead in the northern hemisphere. The interior of northern India is heated intensely. A low pressure air system develops over northern India.

2 **The wet season**   Air is drawn in towards the area of low pressure. The air comes off the sea, and because it is hot it carries lots of water vapour. When the air is forced to rise over the coast (and even more over the Himalayan foothills), it brings very heavy rainfall.

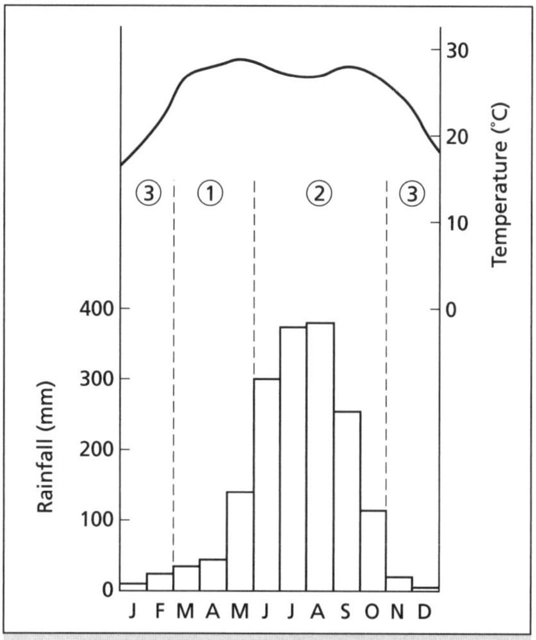

▲ *Figure 13.2 Calcutta's monsoon climate*

3 **The cool dry season**   The sun is overhead in the southern hemisphere. Air over northern India becomes cooler. This forms a high pressure air system. Cool winds blow out from the area of high pressure. The winds are dry because they form over land.

The farmers in the area rely heavily on this pattern of rainfall. Their agricultural calendar is built around the rain, the floods, and irrigation water brought by the rivers. If the rains are early the preparation of the fields may not be complete, causing problems for the farmers.

The problems are worse when the rains are late, or when less rain falls than expected. Then the season can be cut short and yields can be lower than needed. When yields fall, subsistence farmers may have to take out loans, at high interest, so that they can buy food to survive. Shortages drive up the price of rice, causing even greater problems for subsistence farmers and for the poor in the towns.

Hints and Tips!

Do not think of India's climate in terms of spring, summer, autumn and winter. These terms will only confuse you. Use the names of the three seasons given in the text.

Flooding in the Ganges basin – physical factors

Rainfall is concentrated in the period between April and September, and so the rivers regularly flood after the period of heavy rainfall. Farmers rely on the floods to provide water for the crops and sediment to fertilise the fields. In the dry season, rivers fall to low levels.

Cyclones

Cyclones can also cause flooding at certain times of the year.

● A lot of the precipitation in the Himalayas falls as snow. This builds up during the winter, then melts during the thaw. Meltwater can cause floods downstream.

- Between August and October, tropical cyclones form over the Bay of Bengal. They blow in towards the coast of Bangladesh and north-east India. They bring heavy rain and tidal surges, which both increase the flood risk in the lower valley and the delta.

The causes of cyclones

Cyclones form:

- over the sea

- when the temperature of the water is at least 27°C

- towards the end of the hot season when the sea is at its hottest

- in the areas around 20° north or south of the Equator.

    - The air in contact with the hot sea becomes heated.
    - It is able to pick up a lot of moisture, by evaporation.
    - The air starts to rise and condensation takes place, releasing latent heat into the air.
    - The release of heat makes the air rise even faster.
    - Fresh air is drawn in, at sea level, to take the place of the rising air.
    - This, in turn, is heated and rises.
    - As more air rushes in it starts to circulate around the centre of the cyclone, because of the rate of the spin of the earth at that latitude.
    - The whole cyclone, which can be 400 km across, often moves from sea towards the land.
    - In the Bay of Bengal the shape of the coast often funnels cyclones towards the coast around the Ganges delta.

All this produces:

- very heavy rain, from the convection that has been set up

- very strong winds from the in-rush and circulation of air

- large waves whipped up by the wind

- a surge of water, because the low pressure in the cyclone sucks up the sea's surface so that it can be two metres higher than normal

- a stronger surge of water happens in the Bay of Bengal as the shape of the coast concentrates the rising water into the delta area.

The effects of cyclones

Two of the most disastrous cyclones to hit the Ganges delta struck in 1970 and 1985. In 1970 a storm surge wave over 8m high flooded the delta. 300 000 people died, and 1 million were left homeless.

An even bigger wave struck in 1985. Estimated at 9m in height, it flooded 150km inland across the flat delta. Only 40 000 people lost their lives this time, but an enormous relief effort had to be mounted.

- In the **short term** it was important to try to rescue as many of the people stranded by the waves as possible. This was difficult because almost all the area's roads and railways had been cut. Helicopters and boats were the only ways of reaching the survivors.

When the monsoon causes the Ganges to flood, the water usually rises slowly and predictably. People can prepare for the flood. Tropical storms are usually sudden and far less predictable. Therefore the floods they bring can cause far more damage.

- In the **medium term** it was vital to prevent an outbreak of typhoid. The flood had contaminated water supplies with sewage and dead bodies. Disease could have spread very rapidly if it once became established.

- In the **long term** the people had to be fed. The flood had destroyed the rice crop and contaminated the soil with salt water. People needed emergency food supplies, but they also needed help to reclaim their land, replace lost cattle and rebuild their ruined fishing boats.

Managing the effects of cyclones

Cyclones contain absolutely enormous amounts of energy. It is impossible for people to control such powerful forces, but careful management can reduce their damaging effects by:

- long-term planning in areas where storms are common

- studying and tracking storms once they form

- action as the storm approaches, to minimise damage.

Planning for cyclones in Bangladesh

The Flood Action Plan (FAP) is an attempt by the Bangladeshi authorities and international aid donors to tackle the area's problems. Projects that are being researched, and which may be built over the next 30 years, include:

- improved satellite weather forecasting, to allow better prediction

- reinforcing coastal banks to protect land and people from floods

- raising the mounds that people live on, so that they are above the level of the highest floods

- improving roads so that aid can be delivered more easily

- building concrete storm shelters.

Flooding in the Ganges basin – human factors

In this section it is important to ask three questions about the interrelationship between the rivers and the people.

1 Are human activities increasing flooding?

In many parts of the catchment area of the Ganges, deforestation is taking place. People clear trees for farmland, and to provide fuelwood and building material. It seems certain that this has led to increased flooding in parts of Nepal and Bhutan, close to where the clearance has taken place. This is a result of:

- less **interception** of rainfall by plant leaves

- less **infiltration** of water into the soil, because land that is not protected by vegetation gets baked hard by the sun

- less **take-up** of water by plant roots

Focus Point 1

List four aspects of the human and physical geography of Bangladesh that make tropical storms here particularly dangerous.

List four ways of reducing the damage done by cyclones in Bangladesh's Flood Action Plan.

Focus Point 2

Give three reasons why deforestation can increase flooding down-stream.

- more **erosion** of soil, because it is no longer bound together by plant roots. This leads to deposition of sediment on the flood plains, blocking rivers.

At the same time, there has been an increase in the number of cyclones coming from the Bay of Bengal. They have also caused greater damage and loss of life, because population growth means more people are now forced to live on the flood plains. The floods cause more death and damage, even though they are no higher than in the past.

2 What about global warming?

The causes and consequences of global warming are explained in chapter 17. One of the consequences is a rise in sea level all over the globe. This will obviously have an enormous effect on a low-lying area such as the Ganges delta, which already suffers regular flooding. Rising sea level can only make the problem worse.

3 How important are the floods to people who live near to the rivers?

The regular, annual flooding is vital to the people who live on the flood plain of the Ganges. People have adapted their lives to the floods. Most people live on mounds of land, above the normal flood level. The roads and tracks are also built along natural or artificial banks.

The farming season is planned around the floods. Rice is the main crop and there are many different varieties. Each is adapted to slight differences in temperature, length of growing season, and depth of the flood water in the fields. The various types are planted in different areas as the flood waters advance and then retreat. Without the floods the very high population densities in this area could not be supported by the land.

Seasonally flooded land also provides feeding grounds for fish. They provide a vital food source for the inhabitants. For many poor people, fish from their fields are their main source of protein.

4 What is being done, and what more could be done, to reduce the damaging effects of the floods?

After the 1988 floods the Bangladesh government and international aid donors set up the Flood Action Plan (FAP). In order to try to control river flooding, banks are being built, or strengthened, along most of the major rivers across the delta and the flood plain. But they are built to allow 'controlled flooding'. Sluice gates allow 'normal' flood water onto the land to irrigate it, but they keep the excess water` in the rivers.

In some areas the FAP is encouraging people to move further away from the river during the flood season. They will only do this if they can grow their crops during the dry season, so the FAP is trying to provide more irrigation water during the dry period.

Other FAP projects include:

- improving flood warning systems

- providing shelters on raised legs, to protect large numbers of people from both river floods and sea floods, caused by cyclones

Note Only people with detailed local knowledge can plan properly to make sure that the FAP meets local needs. As with many projects in LEDCs, outsiders can give useful advice – but they must not ignore local knowledge and just tell people what is best for them.

Some people fear that the spread of high-yielding varieties of rice (HYVs), produced by genetic engineering, could result in some of the specialised local varieties being abandoned.

Focus Point 3

Cover the page then give four examples of ways that the FAP is helping local people to 'live with the floods'.

- raising the mounds that homes are built on, to give extra protection.

In other words, the FAP is helping Bangladeshis to 'live with the floods'.

The subsistence rice growing system

Rice is probably the world's most important food crop. Between one-third and a half of the world's population rely on rice as their staple (main) food. Rice grows best in the monsoon climates of tropical Asia, and over 80 per cent of the world's production is in this region.

Rice grows best with the following inputs from the natural environment:

- a growing season of about 5 months, with temperatures above 21°C

- annual rainfall of over 2000mm, mostly in the growing season

- a dry spell, after the growing season, for harvesting

- flat land, to allow the water to be kept on the fields

- heavy alluvial soils, to provide nutrients

- impermeable soils, to stop the water draining away from the fields.

These conditions are all found on the flood plain of the Ganges. Subsistence farming grew up in this area, based on village units, and this system survived until the late 1950s. Most villages were home to 500–5000 people, including:

- one or two large land-owning families

- several families owning small areas of land

- several families renting land from the large landowners

- landless farmers, who worked for the landowners when possible

- some 'craftsmen families', like blacksmiths, shoemakers and tailors.

Most families farmed on a subsistence basis, each growing enough food for their own use. The larger farmers usually produced a surplus which they sold in the cities, or to visiting merchants. The small farmers produced a surplus in good years, but often they, and the landless farmers, fell into debt in bad years.

There were occasional famines, mainly when monsoon floods were late, but these were usually localised, and did not spread across the whole of India. The railway system allowed emergency food supplies to be taken to areas of shortage in all but the worst years.

However, in the 1950s and 1960s the population was seen to be increasing more quickly than it had done in the past. Famine and mass starvation were a very serious threat in India and Bangladesh. The problem could be tackled, in two different ways.

- reduce population, or at least slow down the growth, and

- increase food production.

Hints and Tips!

Note that in this list of the needs of rice there are no simple statements. Each point has been **elaborated** by adding either a statistic or an explanation. In the exam, simple statements get some marks but you need to elaborate your statements to get the better, high-level marks.

Note When the floods are late, the growing season is cut short. This means that the rice yields are lower than normal. Farmers have to adapt their plans to grow as much as possible in order to survive even in the difficult conditions.

With the help of foreign aid, the main policy was to increase food production through the use of intermediate technology and the more high-technology developments known as the **Green Revolution**.

The Green Revolution in India

The Green Revolution was a group of changes aimed at increasing outputs by increasing inputs. High-tech solutions were developed by scientists, marketed by seed and fertiliser companies, and used by farmers in less economically developed countries. (See Figure 13.3)

The Green Revolution was introduced in the Punjab in the 1960s and worked well there because soil conditions were good, irrigation water was freely available and the farmers were already quite well educated

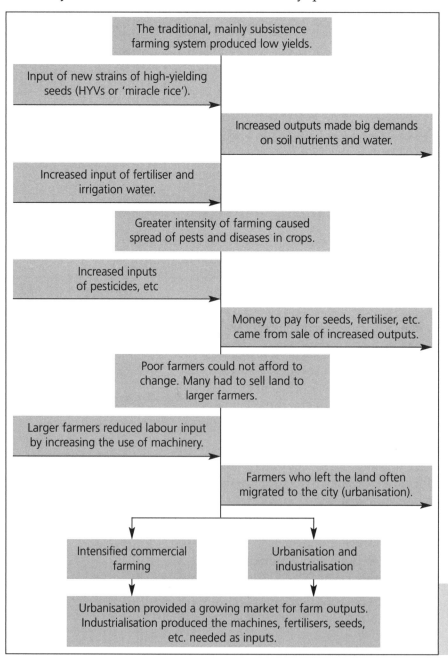

Figure 13.3
The Green Revolution changes

Hints and Tips!

As with many changes, the Green Revolution brought benefits and problems. Make sure that you can write about both in the examination. Aim for balance in your answers.

ocus Point 4

Name four inputs needed by the Green Revolution.

Why did the Green Revolution lead to increased urbanisation?

and progressive. It has spread to other parts of India, including the Ganges delta, but it has not always been so successful there. Farmers have been slower to take on the new technology, and the systems for providing irrigation water are not so well developed as in the Punjab. However, yields are rising slowly but steadily even in this area.

There has been a lot of discussion about the advantages and disadvantages of the changes. Many people suffered, because they could not compete with the new, more capital-intensive farmers. Many lost their land. Some moved to the cities, but others stayed in the countryside looking for occasional work as landless labourers.

However, it is clear now that the famines that were predicted did not happen. India can feed its population. The Green Revolution has now spread to other parts of India. The ideas have often been spread by education programmes carried on satellite TV channels, which have been made available in most Indian villages. Farmers have become better educated and more willing to accept new ideas. As this has happened birth rates have started to fall in rural areas.

Problems still remain. In particular, there is concern that India's farmers are becoming more dependent on fertilisers, fuel and chemicals made from oil products. This may cause serious long-term problems as these become more scarce but, for now at least, the population is being fed and disaster has been averted.

Intermediate technology and farm development

Intermediate technology (IT) developments are very different from the changes brought by the Green Revolution. The idea of IT was developed by Dr E. F. Schumacher. Writing about how development should take place, he said:

> 'If you are poor, start with something cheap.
> If you are uneducated, start with something fairly simple.
> If you are unemployed, start using labour power, because any use of labour is better than letting it lie idle.
> A project that does not fit into the environment will be an economic failure and will cause disruption.' …

> 'Give a man a fish and you feed him for a day; teach him to fish and he can feed himself for a lifetime.' … 'Teach him to make his own fishing tackle and you have helped him to become self-supporting and independent.' …

Intermediate technology supports:

- not large dams … … but wells so that people can pump up enough water for their own fields. These are cheaper, land is not lost to flooding, and local people can control them themselves.

Not a lot of people realise that India is one of the world's leading countries in terms of use of satellites for TV signals.

ActionAid is a charity based in the UK. It works in Bola Island in Bangladesh helping people in communities to drill wells for villages. These have to go down 250m to reach layers of sandstone that are saturated with clean, fresh water. Then they install hand pumps to draw the water to the surface.

- not diesel pumps for the wells …

… but hand-operated pumps, so that local labour is used, rather than expensive, imported fuel. They are also easier to repair, and spare parts can be made in the village.

- not tractors …

… but improved hand tools that can be made from recycled scrap metal by blacksmiths working in the villages.

- not expensive chemical fertilisers …

… but compost made by recycling plant waste and manure.

- not pesticides which pollute the soil …

… but encourage natural predators which eat insects that destroy crops; or teach children to pick pests off the crops.

ocus Point 5

Cover the page. What does intermediate technology support instead of:

- large dams
- diesel pumps
- tractors
- fertilisers
- pesticides?

Exam practice

(a) (i)   How is the land in a delta formed?   (2 marks)

   (ii) What is a distributary?   (1 mark)

   (iii) Why does a delta often provide very fertile soil for farming?   (2 marks)

(b) Cyclones often cause severe flooding in the Ganges delta area.

   (i)   Why have these floods often caused a very high death rate? Refer to:
   - the nature of the cyclones
   - the relief of the land
   - the level of economic development of the area.   (7 marks)

   (ii) Describe one way in which the governments in the area and/or international relief agencies are trying to reduce the damage caused by cyclones.   (3 marks)

The population of India and Bangladesh

In any study of population you need to know some basic terms.

Birth rate   the number of babies born, for every thousand people in a country, in a year. It is expressed as 'live births/thousand/year' or '‰/year'.

Death rate   the number of people dying out of every thousand in a country, in a year. It is expressed as 'deaths/thousand/year' or '‰/year'.

Natural increase   the difference between the number of births and the number of deaths, in a country, in a year. It is usually expressed as a percentage.

Life expectancy   the average age that people in a country live to be. Separate figures are usually given for males and females.

Hints and Tips!

Learn these five definitions precisely.

Infant mortality   the number of babies dying before they reach their fifth birthday. This figure is usually given per thousand population (‰).

Basic population statistics are given below for India and Bangladesh. Figures for the UK are also given for comparison.

	Birth rate (per 1000)	Death rate (per 1000)	Natural increase %	Life expectancy Male (years)	Female (years)	Infant mortality (per 1000)
India	29	10	1.9	57	59	87
Bangladesh	36	13	2.3	54	52	118
UK	14	11	0.3	73	79	7

The demographic transition model

In many countries it has been observed that, as the economy develops, the population structure goes through a series of changes. These changes are called the **demographic transition**.

Stage 1

In countries with very simple, subsistence economies, health care is usually poor. This means that the death rate is high, especially amongst the most vulnerable group – babies and children under five.

Couples usually have many babies, hoping that one or two will survive, so the birth rate is also high.

A high birth rate and a high death rate means that the population stays low. It may fall suddenly in bad years of drought, famine or disease. Then it may rise slowly again as conditions improve, only to fall again when the next difficult time arrives.

Both India and Bangladesh have passed through this stage. Their death rate is now much lower than in Stage 1.

Stage 2

As the economy starts to develop, money becomes available for better health care – doctors, nurses, medicines, better sanitation, drier and warmer housing, better pre- and post-natal care, etc. This means death rate starts to fall, slowly at first, then faster as conditions improve. Usually birth rate stays high, because people are used to having many children. It takes time to change the 'culture of the high birth rate'.

The high birth rate and falling death rate combine to cause population increase. It starts growing slowly, but the rate of growth speeds up. This can cause a 'population explosion'.

Bangladesh and India both entered this stage in the 1950s/1960s. Bangladesh is still in this stage – see the graph above.

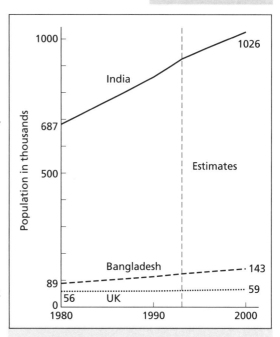

▲ *Figure 13.4 Population changes, 1980–2000 (est.)*

In the 1960s the world's population increased very rapidly. This was not because people had started to have many more children – it was because fewer people were dying.

Stage 3

People keep on having large numbers of children as long as they feel there is a need for them. Reasons for a high birth rate include:

- children can support parents in their old age

- children can work on farms, in industry or in services. Their wages can make the difference between survival and disaster for families.

So the birth rate starts to fall when people no longer feel that they *need* to have large families. In other words, it falls as the standard of living of the poor people starts to rise.

In this stage the death rate is low, and although the birth rate is falling it is still higher than the death rate. The population total still grows, but the rate of growth slows down.

India is probably in Stage 3 now. The birth rate has started to fall. It is still rather high, but it is quite a lot lower than in Bangladesh. Actually this overall figure hides variations. The birth rate in the cities is usually lower than the rate in the countryside. If figures were available to compare the birth rates in Calcutta and in the rice-growing areas of the delta, they would probably show that Calcutta is well into Stage 3 but the rural areas are still in Stage 2.

Stage 4

In most MEDCs birth and death rates are both low. Health care is good and reliable. People expect their children to survive, so they keep families small. In fact, in more wealthy countries children have become very expensive, because people expect to pay for them to have a high standard of housing, food, leisure, etc. People have a strong **motive** to limit their families, and family planning gives them the **means** to do this.

Contraceptives and family planning advice alone will not cut the birth rate. It only falls when couples realise *they* can benefit by not having big families.

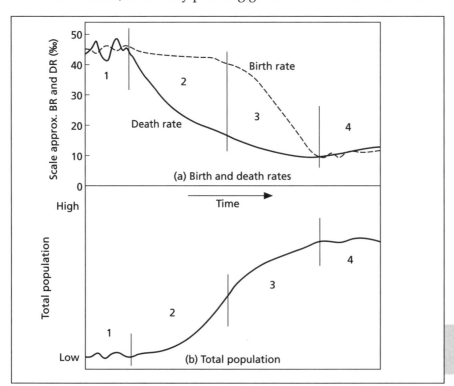

In Stage 3 the population increase slows down – but population is still rising. Unfortunately students often get confused about this and say that population starts to fall. BE CAREFUL! Do not make this mistake.

◀ *Figure 13.5 The demographic transition model*

In MEDCs, with a low birth and death rate, the total population is steady. Total population is often high, but these countries have a strong economy, which can support the large numbers. The UK is now in Stage 4.

Population policies

Careful study of the details of the demographic transition model above should make one thing clear. *It seems as though the most reliable way to reduce the birth rate is to raise people's standard of living.* There are many reasons why poor peasant farmers need to have many children.

- Children can work on the farm from a very early age. Even 6 and 7-year-olds can help to scare birds or weed the crops.

- Children are needed to support their parents in old age. There are no old age pensions.

- With the high death rate, parents feel that they need to have many children so that they can be sure that at least one will survive.

- At least one of the children may be able to get work in a city and send money home to support the family.

- People take great pride in their families, and sons often play an important part in religious ceremonies, including the Hindu funeral ceremonies.

In India there have been several big campaigns to try to encourage people to use contraception. The government and aid agencies tried various policies.

- Advertising the benefits of smaller families, using posters, TV and even, in one famous example, painting slogans on the side of elephants and leading them round villages.

- Giving away free contraceptives – but this is no use unless couples want to use them and know how to use them. Contraceptive education is difficult in areas where many people are illiterate and the education of women is especially poor.

- Encouraging men to be sterilised, at first by persuasion, and then by forcing some men to be sterilised. This caused widespread opposition, and was one reason why the government of the time was voted out of power. Democratic India would not accept the kind of policies that had worked in China.

- Recently it has been found that the best way to cut the birth rate is to educate and support women. In particular to:
  - provide good health care for women and their children
  - encourage literacy, so that women can read advice on health care, contraception, good diet, and so on
  - raise the status of women, so they can control their own lives and make decisions about their families.

Focus Point 6

Cover up the page. Give at least four reasons why poor farming families in India and Bangladesh need to have a lot of children.

It is useful to compare China's one-child policy with India's slower but kinder policy. Their birth rate is falling because people are starting to realise that their living conditions *can* get better, but only if they cut family size.

Focus Point 7

Cover the page. List three ways of working with women to help create the right conditions that will lead to a fall in the birth rate.

There is now clear evidence that India's population growth is starting to slow down. This is happening fastest in the cities and in those rural areas where the farming is most developed. Unfortunately, the growth rate is still high in Bangladesh. The country is poorer, with less money to spend on health care and education.

Exam practice

(a) The population of the rural areas of the Ganges delta has a high birth rate.

  (i)   Give two reasons to explain why the birth rate is so high in this area.   (4 marks)

  (ii) Some people say that the best way to cut the birth rate is to improve health care for babies and children. Why is this so?   (2 marks)

(b) (i) Complete this table to show changes during the demographic transition. (You may use words from the list below, but Higher-level candidates should not need to use them.)

Stage	1	2	3	4
Death rate				
Birth rate				
Total population				

          (8 marks)

  - high • high • high but now stable • low • low • low
  - rising at an increasing rate • starts to fall • starts to fall • stays high
  - still falling • still rising, but at slower rate

  (ii) Explain what causes the change from Stage 2 to Stage 3 of the demographic transition.   (2 marks)

  (iii) Explain what causes the change from Stage 3 to Stage 4.   (2 marks)

14 Japan: urbanisation and industrialisation in a resource-poor environment

For this topic you should study:
- location of the four main islands and the major settlements
- the main physical features, and their influence on the distribution of population and industry
- location of natural resources and the need for imports of raw materials
- production of manufactured goods, with particular reference to:
  - factors affecting the distribution of the motor vehicle and electronics industries
  - environmental damage and pollution, and attempted solutions to the problems.

Japan's physical features and population distribution

Japan lies on the margin between the Pacific Plate and the Eurasian Plate. This is a destructive margin, where the denser Pacific Plate is being forced down beneath the continental Eurasian Plate. This violent movement causes earthquakes and volcanoes which have formed the mountains of Japan.

The friction between the plates also generates heat. This can cause the ocean plate to melt as it sinks down into the mantle. The melting produces a reservoir of magma (molten rock) beneath the Earth's crust. Sometimes the pressure on this magma forces it upwards, through a crack in the crust. Then it spills out at the surface as a volcano.

Mountains, deep river valleys and the rocky, unstable coastline make large parts of Japan unsuitable for human settlement. Only 17 per cent of the land is suitable for dense settlement and industry. This is almost all found on the narrow coastal strip. Settlements are particularly concentrated around the bays and inlets which form sheltered harbours, because so many people depend on the industries that have grown up there, based on imported raw materials.

The bays also provide some shelter from tsunamis and typhoons, which are other natural hazards that threaten Japan. **Tsunamis** are great waves, set off by earthquakes on the sea bed. They can affect any part of Japan, but especially the east coast. **Typhoon** is the local name for tropical storms, similar to the cyclones in the Bay of Bengal (see page 104). Typhoons are common in Kyushu and southern Honshu.

Japan's natural resources

Compared with other major industrial countries, Japan is very short of natural resources. For instance:

- **Coal** – When Japan first started to industrialise in the late nineteenth century, there were some small, poor deposits in the south of the country and on Hokkaido, but now these are just about exhausted.

There is no English word for 'tsunami'. These waves are sometimes called 'tidal waves', but they have nothing to do with the tides, so it is better just to borrow from the Japanese and call them tsunami.

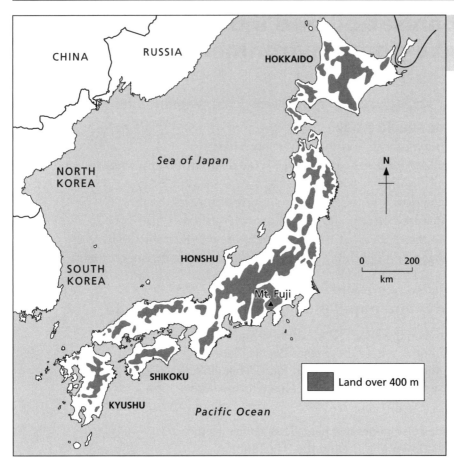

Hints and Tips!

◆ To help
remember why
there are
earthquakes at plate
margins think of the
three stages:

1 **Movement**
caused by
convection current.

2 **Friction** between
the plates.

3 **Sudden slip**
when pressure
builds up, causes
earthquake.

◆ To help
remember why
volcanoes erupt at
plate margins, think
of three stages:

1 Heavier plate
sinks as they move
together.

2 Sinking plate
melts due to
friction and heating.

3 **Pressure build-
up** causes eruption.

● **Oil and gas** – Some fields have also been found on Honshu, but
these have never been important.

● **HEP** – Japan's high mountains, steep slopes and reliable rainfall, all
favour HEP. Unfortunately, none of the river basins are large enough
to allow the development of major schemes. HEP provides 7 per
cent of Japan's electricity at present, but this is unlikely to increase.
The biggest HEP scheme is on the Kurobe River.

● **Geothermal power** – At present, 5 per cent of Japan's electricity
comes from geothermal schemes . Many of the rocks below the
surface are hot, so there is a lot of potential for further development.

● **Alternative power** – Like Britain, Japan is an island, surrounded by
seas where strong winds blow, waves are high and the range of the
tides in some of the bays is great. All of this offers potential for
generation of electricity in the twenty-first century. It has not been
developed yet, but Japan may prove to have better energy resources
in the next century than it has had in the past!

Manufacturing industry in Japan

From reading the previous section you will realise that most of Japan's
raw materials for industry have to be imported.

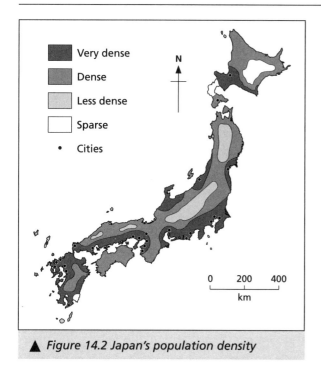

▲ Figure 14.2 Japan's population density

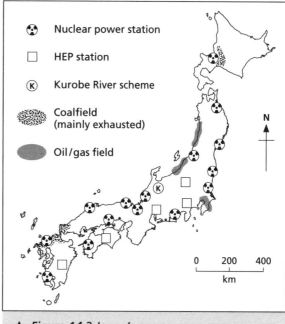

▲ Figure 14.3 Japan's energy resources

Japan could only industrialise by making sure that:

- it could afford to pay for the imports by exporting lots of goods
- its exports were high value compared with low-value imports
- it controlled the sources of supply of its imports.

To control supplies of essential raw materials, Japan often invested in mines, railways and ports in other countries.

You should now be able to work out two main reasons why Japanese industry is concentrated around the coast:

- Most people live close to the coast because of the flat land. These people provide the workforce and the market.
- Most raw materials are brought in through the ports, so transport costs are reduced if the factory is close to the coast.

	Imports that Japan needs
Uranium	100%
Iron ore (although now a lot of scrap is reused)	100%
Oil	99.8%
Gas	99.5%
Hard wood	95%
Coal	88%

Industry is concentrated in the four main industrial zones shown on Figure 14.4 on page 118.

An example of Japanese investment in other countries to provide raw materials for Japan's industry is the iron ore mine at Mt Tom Price in the north-west of Australia. This was built entirely by the Japanese, and all the ore is exported to Japan.

ocus Point 1

Cover up the page. Give the two main reasons why Japan's industry is concentrated around the coast.

The motor industry

In Japan there are two parts to the motor industry:

- A few very large, highly automated, capital-intensive assembly plants. The locations of the main plants are shown on Figure 14.5.

- Many small, more labour-intensive component manufacturers. They are mostly found in the main industrial areas, but others are scattered throughout the country.

For example, many firms in the Kobe region make parts for larger firms throughout Japan. The country's efficient transport system means that these parts can be delivered very quickly, 'just in time' to be used in production. Big firms therefore do not need to hold large stocks of parts. One unexpected result of the Kobe earthquake in 1995 was the damage done to the motor industry. The earthquake disrupted many of Kobe's firms, and the whole region's transport system. Without parts from Kobe, many of the big factories had to stop work for several weeks, even months.

The motor industry uses steel as its main raw material, so the main engine and body plants are located close to steel works, which are close to the ports. New car assembly plants are often built on land that has been reclaimed from the sea, because of the shortage of suitable flat land.

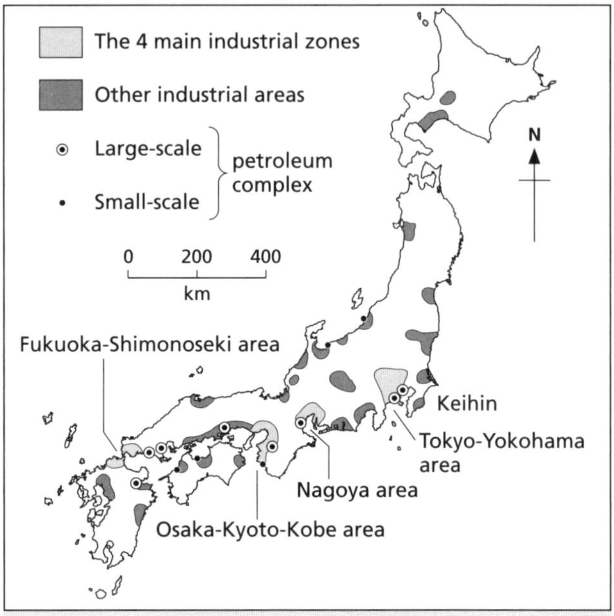

The electronics industry

Refer back to the section on 'High-technology industry in the M4 corridor' on pages 45–46. This makes the point that high-tech industry can be divided into two sections. These deal with research and development, and mass production of the goods. Exactly the same situation can be found in Japan's high-tech industry.

Stage 1 – research and development   The electronics, optical (cameras, etc.) and computer industries in Japan are enormous, and play a vital part in their economy. The high-tech sector first developed in the late 1950s and 1960s. Then the Japanese took ideas that had been developed in the West and used them efficiently to make more profits than the people who had the original ideas. Now, a lot of the profits made by the big firms are re-invested in research and development.

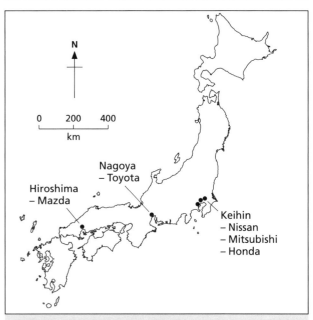

The 4 main industrial zones

Other industrial areas

⊙ Large-scale ⎫
              ⎬ petroleum complex
· Small-scale ⎭

0   200   400
        km

Fukuoka-Shimonoseki area

Keihin

Tokyo-Yokohama area

Nagoya area

Osaka-Kyoto-Kobe area

▲ Figure 14.4 Japan's industrial zones

0   200   400
        km

Nagoya – Toyota

Hiroshima – Mazda

Keihin
– Nissan
– Mitsubishi
– Honda

▲ Figure 14.5 Location of Japan's major car assembly plants

Tsukuba Science City

Tsukuba Science City lies 20km north-east of the edge of Tokyo and 20km north-west of the Narita International Airport. It is right on the line of the bullet train. It is an area of beautiful countryside, and has attracted some of the best brains in Japan to work there.

It contains research institutes for:

- higher level physics
- disaster prevention
- engineering and minerals
- electronics
- automobiles
- agriculture and forestry.

There are also libraries, exhibition centres and universities. It has areas of landscaped business and science parks to attract high-tech industries of a variety of sizes and scales.

This concentration of research expertise, beautiful environment, excellent national and international communications networks and access to the biggest market in Asia has made Tsukuba into a major centre of the Japanese electronics industry. Many Japanese firms and foreign owned trans-nationals have located in this area. (Compare this area with the M4 corridor, described on pages 45–46.)

Stage 2 – manufacturing in Japan Once the ideas have been developed, the products are built in other parts of Japan. As with the motor industry, large corporations build assembly plants, usually near big cities, close to labour and the market. The components are made in small factories and workshops scattered around the country.

Stage 3 – manufacturing overseas Labour in Japan is expensive, and it is likely to become more expensive. Skilled workers expect good wages and benefits. They can demand good conditions, because there is a growing shortage of workers as the population ages.

The big corporations try to cut down costs by:

- mechanisation – replacing workers with machinery
- encouraging hard work from the labour force – providing good conditions, but expecting dedicated work in exchange.

In spite of this it is difficult to stay competitive with countries where labour costs are lower. As a result Japanese corporations are now building factories overseas. Once they have shown that their production processses can be successful and their goods are profitable, the major electronic firms produce most of their goods in countries

Focus **Point 2**

Describe three stages in the location of the Japanese high-tech industry. Use these headings:

1 Research and development
2 Early production
3 Later, mass production

where labour is cheaper. Many 'Japanese' electronic goods – computers, game consoles and so on – are actually assembled in countries like Malaysia and Thailand – the 'tiger economies'. In the late 1990s they spread into even poorer countries, such as Bangladesh and India. This leads to:

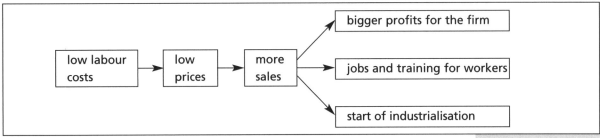

▲ Figure 14.6

Japanese industry and the environment

The rapid development of industry in a small, crowded country, where only a small percentage of the land is suitable for settlement, has led to many environmental problems.

For instance:

- Tokyo Bay became very badly polluted with waste from the steel and chemical works built around the bay. Air pollution was also caused by the burning of rubbish in giant incinerators and by exhaust fumes from the traffic.

- Lake Biwa, in the centre of the country, was made sterile by industrial waste, untreated sewage and excess fertiliser washed off farmland.

- Minamata Bay in the extreme south-west of the country was polluted by mercury in waste from the nearby chemical works.

The Japanese, as might be expected, have shown great ingenuity in attempting to tackle the problems.

Other problems and solutions have included:

Hints and Tips!

Learn the list of problems first. Once you know them it is far easier to learn the solutions, because you have a structure to help your learning.

Problem	Solution
Exhaustion of fuel resources.	Development of nuclear power and HEP. Research into alternatives, like solar and geothermal power.
Deforestation of Japan's countryside.	Replanting of forest on steep slopes. Setting up National Parks to conserve remaining forests.
Shortage of land for industry	Building new land into the sea, often using rubbish to fill in part of the site.
Waste from factories	Water sprinklers reduce dust released from piles of raw materials. Treatment and recycling of waste products reduces output of pollution. Chemical treatment of waste from power station and factory chimneys reduces output of acids.

Problem	Solution
Fumes from incinerators	Chimneys built much higher so that waste gases are released into higher atmosphere and do not fall back to surface until out over the Pacific.
Car exhausts	Still a problem, but research into smaller, more efficient engines is ongoing, public transport is improving to reduce car use, and the use of lead-free petrol and the reduction of other additives in petrol reduces the toxicity of fumes.
Mercury pollution	Very strict laws, careful monitoring and heavy fines or even closure of polluting plants.
Untreated sewage	Massive investment in sewage treatment works.
Pollution by farms	Research into exact needs of different crops and different soils has reduced chemical inputs into farming, cut farmers' costs and reduced pollution.

Exam practice

(a) (i) Name two important forms of energy for which Japan has to rely on importing most of its supplies. (1 mark)

(ii) Name two alternative (renewable) sources of energy that Japan can produce for itself (or may soon be able to produce). (1 mark)

(iii) Choose one of the sources of alternative energy named in (ii) above. Explain why the land of Japan is suitable for production of this type of energy. (3 marks)

(b) (i) Name one of Japan's major industrial regions and mark it on an outline map of the country. (1 mark)

(ii) Give two reasons to explain why most of Japan's industry is located on the coast. (4 marks)

(iii) In the past, Japanese industry had a reputation for copying other people's ideas and not developing its own. This is no longer true. Explain what the Japanese are doing to encourage research and development (R&D) for industry. (2 marks)

Global issues

15 Population growth and urbanisation

For this topic you should study:
- a comparison of the population in one LEDC with that in one MEDC
- the consequences of rapid population growth in LEDCs, including urbanisation
- the world pattern of urbanisation
- the push/pull model of urbanisation
- the development of squatter settlements and the informal sector of the economy in one large urban area
- attempts to improve conditions in squatter settlements, including self-help schemes and schemes managed by the authorities.

Population structures

In chapter 13 we looked at population totals and changes in total population. Geographers also need to look at the **structure** of the population. This means examining how the population can be divided up into different groups, based on age and sex. The usual way of showing this information is on a **population pyramid**.

▼ *Figure 15.1 Population pyramids for India, Bangladesh and the UK*

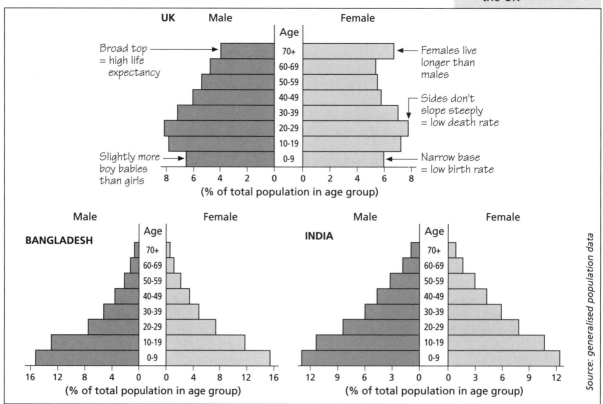

Source: generalised population data

In the pyramids, each bar represents an age/sex group. Males are shown on the left and females on the right; young people are at the bottom and old people at the top. The length of the bar shows the percentage of the total population in that group. For instance, in India 13.7 per cent of the total population is male, from 0–9 years old.

The consequences of rapid population growth

The growth of population in both India and Bangladesh is more rapid in the countryside than in urban areas. You must remember that people have large families because they need them (see page 113). However, the rapid growth of the total rural population has some damaging effects on the rural area as a whole.

The most important damaging effect of the population growth is a demand for more food, more land to farm and more jobs. The pressures cause a push leading to urbanisation.

Migration to cities

Conditions in rural areas put a lot of pressures on the inhabitants to leave the countryside and migrate to the cities. These pressures are sometimes called **pushes**. The diagram below shows some of them.

Focus Point 1

Annotate either the Bangladesh or the India pyramid, to show how it is different from the UK pyramid.

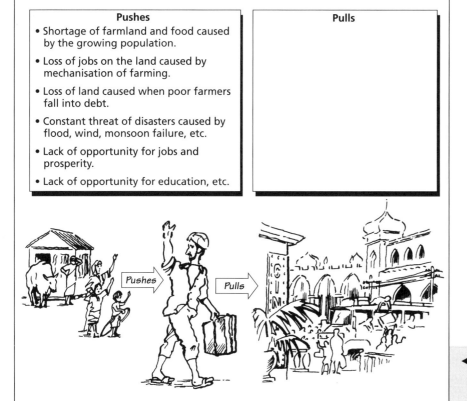

Pushes	Pulls
• Shortage of farmland and food caused by the growing population. • Loss of jobs on the land caused by mechanisation of farming. • Loss of land caused when poor farmers fall into debt. • Constant threat of disasters caused by flood, wind, monsoon failure, etc. • Lack of opportunity for jobs and prosperity. • Lack of opportunity for education, etc.	

Focus Point 2

At the same time, the cities often **pull** people towards them. Complete the second half of this diagram by listing some of the pull factors that attract people to Calcutta. Some of these are mentioned on page 125.

◀ Figure 15.2 Countryside to cities: push and pull factors

Urbanisation: the growth of Calcutta

Calcutta, which has a population of about 13 million, is India's second largest city after Bombay, now known as Mumbai (about 16 million). New Delhi, the capital, has about 12 million people.

Calcutta lies on the Hooghly River, which is one of the distributaries carrying water from the Ganges, into the Bay of Bengal. It lies over 100km from the coast, but the Hooghly is so wide that ocean-going boats can reach the city. Calcutta lies on the eastern (left) bank of the river, and forms a conurbation with Howrah on the right bank.

There was a very important trading city and port here in 1757, when the British seized it. They wanted Calcutta so that they could control the trade of Bengal. The area of Bengal probably had around 40 million inhabitants, and the farmers produced a surplus of crops, especially cotton and jute, which were traded for British manufactured goods.

Bengal was the name given to a state that was independent before the British arrived. East Bengal is now the country of Bangladesh. West Bengal is now part of India.

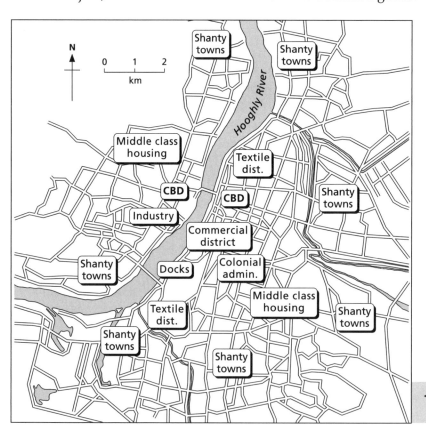

Jute is a plant that produces fibres used to make sacks and rope. Fair trade organisations like 'People Tree' sell items made from jute by poor communities in the Ganges delta region.

◀ *Figure 15.3 Urban zones of Calcutta*

Once the British controlled the city, their merchants built docks, warehouses, company offices, large houses, etc. in the central area. Nearby were the palaces and public buildings of the Indian rulers. The Indian commercial and small industrial areas were further back from the river. They were surrounded by the homes of the people who worked in the city. Calcutta was an important trading port, and it grew steadily. When the British left India in 1947, it had about 2 million people!

Since 1947 there have been many influxes of refugees caused by:

- the riots following the partition of India and Pakistan

- droughts and floods in the region

- people being forced off the land by the commercialisation of agriculture after the Green Revolution in the 1960s and 1970s

- population pressure caused by a high birth rate and falling death rate.

Each new group is pulled to Calcutta by the hope of finding work and shelter. Many of the newcomers have friends and family in Calcutta already, and they look to them for help to get established in the city. Then, even if they cannot find work, they have more chance to make a living by begging in a big city than they could in the countryside.

Many of the refugees set up shanty towns on spare land around the outskirts of Calcutta. Others were forced to live on the pavements in the city centre, moving to live on railway station platforms, in bus shelters and in the entrance halls of large buildings during the monsoon rains.

Growth of the shanty towns ('bustees') in Calcutta

Each new group of migrants either moves to the pavements in the centre, or to spare areas of land on the outskirts. To people from MEDCs, conditions in these settlements looks appalling – but it is vital that you understand why and how these settlements developed.

Most people are attracted to Calcutta by opportunity. Many cannot get formal jobs, but they can make a living in the informal sector. (This does not just mean shoe shining. It includes a great variety of work, buying and selling, making and mending, servicing and recycling.) The chances of an education for their children offers a further opportunity for the family to get on. People in this situation have to be flexible and adapt to change if they are to prosper. They need a home, not luxury.

Informal employment in Calcutta's squatter settlements
Informal employment usually takes place on the streets, or in the same rooms where people live. There are no set hours, no set wages, no formal training, and usually no tax is paid which means there are no benefits if people cannot work.

Informal jobs done by residents of squatter settlements in Calcutta include:

- washing and ironing clothes for richer people (these people are called 'dhobi wallahs')

- street sellers, often selling food brought in from the person's home village in the countryside

- building and maintaining huts in the settlement

- collecting, sorting and re-selling scrap material

Hints and Tips!
In the exam, do not just say 'they came to work'. What kind of work did they look for? You know Calcutta has docks and industries, shops and offices. There would be some jobs there, but most new migrants would have to look for very menial work – street cleaning, sorting and recycling rubbish, selling things on the street, domestic work, and so on.

- letter writing, for illiterate neighbours

- making and selling furniture and household goods like pots and pans – often using recycled materials

- repairing and servicing computers and other electrical equipment (Yes, really!)

- sweeping streets – to be paid by the owners of houses on the street.

Many GCSE students write about 'spontaneous settlements' with a very stereotyped view of the squalor and poverty. They often miss out reasons for the conditions that they describe.

Most new settlements are gradually improved as people can afford to buy materials and improve their homes. The Calcutta Metropolitan Development Authority (CMDA) is responsible for improving conditions in the city. This is happening slowly but surely. Its priority is to provide services, not to improve the houses: that must be left to the occupiers. Since the 1960s the CMDA has:

- improved sewage disposal – in the 1960s there were 1000 deaths a year from cholera but in recent years there have been none

- improved water supply – there is now a tap for every 25 slum houses

- made concrete roads to replace mud tracks between the shacks

Focus Point 3

Cover the page.

List five improvements that the CMDA has made to life in the shanty towns of Calcutta.

Focus Point 4

Cover up the page.

Give five negative stereotypes of spontaneous settlements.

Give the reasons why settlements develop like this.

Negative stereotype	Actual reasons
• Houses are poorly built, often using scrap materials.	• Money is in short supply. It has to be spent on food, or invested in tools or materials for work.
• Houses seem to be poorly planned, with bits tacked on.	• Homes have to provide a place for the family to sleep and eat – and the family may change size as children are born or leave to work elsewhere. Also, people from the home village may need support when they arrive in the city.
• There are no proper windows, and walls are very flimsy.	• Calcutta is in the tropics. Ventilation is more important than insulation.
• The houses do not have proper toilets and sewers.	• These are expensive and complicated. They may be provided in the future, but people often make pit latrines which are emptied by tank lorries every few months.
• They do not have electricity.	• Once settlements are established the authorities may link them to the supply – but it is difficult to keep up with the rapid growth.
• There are no roads, only dirt tracks.	• Not many people own cars. It is more important to have access to a bus route to the city centre.
• The area looks a mess.	• Many people are carrying on their jobs in and around their homes. Builders have to store materials, some keep animals for food, others make things from recycled scrap to sell, and so on. Opportunity is more important than tidiness.

- installed street lights in many shanty towns, to improve safety, and to give some light for people with no electricity in their home

- tried to improve the traffic flow by widening roads and improving public transport. Despite the improvements the traffic system is still very overcrowded (but that problem is not unique to Calcutta).

The CMDA's job has become easier because migration to the city has slowed down. The city's population is now growing by only 0.4 per cent per year (compared with 7 per cent in Mumbai). This is due to:

- Industry is developing in other towns nearby, in the Damodar Valley, providing another attraction to migrants.

- It is now known that Calcutta cannot provide jobs for new migrants and this discourages people who were thinking of moving there.

- Conditions in the countryside have improved. The Green Revolution has improved yields and raised rural living standards.

The world pattern of urbanisation

Urbanisation means the movement of people from rural to urban areas. The **urbanisation of a country** means a growing proportion of a country's population lives in cities.

The map (Figure 15.4) shows the percentage of the population in each country which lives in urban areas. It does not show where urbanisation is taking place now. In fact it shows past urbanisation.

Hints and Tips!

In other words, the pushes from the countryside have got weaker, and the pulls to Calcutta have also got weaker.

Hints and Tips!

You should try not to use stereotypes when you describe spontaneous settlements. Learn precise facts about the CMDA and then you can describe a real place, not just a stereotype slum.

▼ *Figure 15.4 Global patterns of urbanisation*

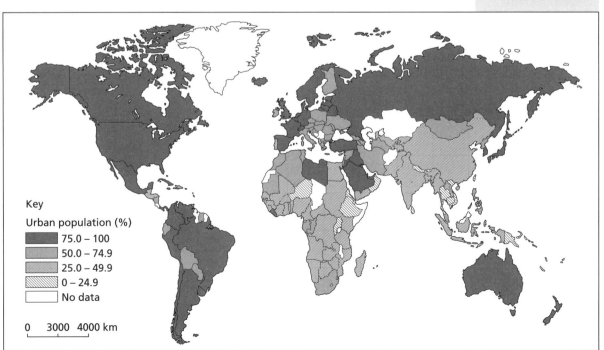

Key

Urban population (%)
- 75.0 – 100
- 50.0 – 74.9
- 25.0 – 49.9
- 0 – 24.9
- No data

0 3000 4000 km

The pattern of world urbanisation may look complicated but it is actually quite easy to see a pattern. The three main themes are described below.

- Most MEDCs in Europe, North America, Japan and Australasia became urbanised in the nineteenth century and the first 70 years or so of the twentieth century. They are now going through a process of counter-urbanisation as people leave cities and move to the countryside or rural-urban fringe.

- Most of Latin America went through the process of urbanisation in the twentieth century. Urbanisation is slowing down now, because there are few people left to move from rural to urban areas.

- Africa, south of the Sahara, and South East Asia are shown to have less than 50 per cent of their population in urban areas – **but it is these areas which are urbanising most quickly at present**.

Exam practice

In Less Economically Developed Countries, many people from rural areas might migrate to cities.

(i)   Name a city in an LEDC which is receiving many migrants.

(ii)   Describe two push factors and two pull factors that help to cause this migration.   (4 marks)

16 Aid, investment and international development

For this topic you should study:
- the types of international aid
- the scale of international aid compared with the needs of the LEDCs
- **one** development project in an LEDC
- the role of international aid donors in encouraging sustainable development
- the role of trans-national corporations in international development – Japanese investment in the EU and the Pacific Rim countries.

Types of aid

There are many types of aid, money or goods sent from richer countries to poorer countries. You need to know the following definitions:

- **Official aid** is money sent from the government of one or more richer countries. It can include:
  - **bilateral aid** which is money sent from one country to another
  - **multilateral aid** when the money comes from a group of countries, usually through an organisation like the World Bank.

- **Voluntary aid** comes from individuals or organisations, such as Oxfam or Action Aid. It also includes aid from religious groups such as Christian Aid, the Red Crescent and Cafod.

Both official aid and voluntary aid can be given in two forms:

- **Short-term aid** is given to help deal with an immediate problem or disaster. It often comes in the form of food, tents, medicine and help with searching for survivors of a disaster such as an earthquake, etc.

- **Long-term aid** is given to help people with long-term development plans, such as improving agriculture, drilling down to the water table to provide clean water, or educating people so that they can get jobs and improve their quality of life.

One form of official aid which has been much publicised recently is **debt relief**. In the past rich countries made loans to poorer countries to help with their development. The recipients of the loans have had to pay interest and then pay back all or part of the loan. Many countries have been unable to pay the interest. They have been forced to spend more and more of their revenue paying money back to the rich countries – so they were unable to spend their income on education, health and long-term development. As part of the millennium celebrations in 2000 some countries 'wrote off' their debts to poor countries. This was a very valuable form of aid – but much more remains to be done.

Hints and Tips!

As this is being written, the Johannesburg Conference on Sustainable Development is taking place. What was the result? Did it affect aid and development policies? Keep up to date. Information on this could be very useful in your exam.

There are some problems with aid donations, especially official aid. These include:

- official aid often comes in the form of new loans, which have to be repaid

- aid may have 'strings attached' in that it has to be spent in the way the donor demands. It may have to be spent on goods or services from the donor country, or on arms, or on projects which will benefit the donor in political and strategic ways

- official aid usually only goes to friendly countries who have political systems which the donor likes.

- money may be kept by corrupt officials or politicians in the receiving country.

The needs of the LEDCs compared with the scale of aid

Some years ago Oxfam published an advert which tried to show that the rich countries were not as generous with their aid payments as they sometimes tried to make out. It said:

> **For every £1 we give in aid to poor countries......**
>
> **....we receive £2 in interest, dividends and repayments.**

Since that advert was published the situation has probably got worse. The proportion of our GNP which is given as aid has fallen. The gap between the GNP per person in the rich and the poor countries has widened during the last few decades.

The United Nations has said that all rich countries should try to pay at least 0.7 per cent of their GNP to poor countries in the form of aid. In fact, very few countries even approach that figure. For example, look at the table on the right.

Country	% of GNP spent on aid
Denmark	0.95
Norway	0.87
Netherlands	0.80
Sweden	0.79
France	0.45
Canada	0.32
Switzerland	0.32
Finland	0.31
Germany	0.29
UK	0.27
Japan	0.24
USA	0.09

ActionAid projects in Bangladesh

ActionAid is a UK-based charity which works in many countries, including Bangladesh. The projects which they support are:

- long-term aid

- usually small-scale projects which are locally based

- mainly run by local people rather than by outsiders.

ActionAid's work in Bangladesh includes the following projects (but you need only learn details of one for the exam).

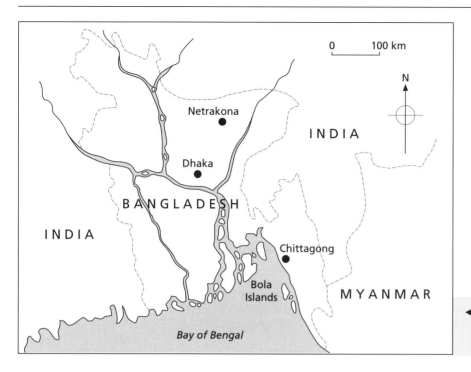

Figure 16.1 The work of ActionAid in Bangladesh

Financing savings groups for village women in Netrakona.
The 'shomiti' is a traditional meeting for women in villages in this area. The women meet to discuss local problems and what they can do to help themselves. ActionAid helps by making money available for them to develop their ideas. The women do not want charity – but they do want to be able to help themselves.

ActionAid provided a loan to help a local woman, Begum Rokeya, run a village primary school, which also held literacy classes for women. This was very successful, so further loans were made to help Begum Rokeya train women from other nearby villages so that they could set up their own schools. As adult women have been taught to read and write they have become much more able to take part in the running of the shomiti credit groups.

One woman used her loan to buy some ducks and set up an enterprise selling eggs and ducklings. This provides a source of protein for the villagers. She can keep the ducks on the edges of the rice fields, where they help to control pests. She can also work and earn money without leaving home – a very important consideration for a woman in a Moslem country.

Other loans have been used to set up enterprises in fish faming, keeping hens, tailoring, batik printing of cloth, bee keeping – and running the shops which sell the products of these enterprises.

However, the main thing that the shomiti groups wanted to invest in was making toilets! People set up businesses making simple concrete toilets with S-bends. When these were fitted into simple shelters they made conditions more hygienic, and much more dignified than the traditional squat.

Focus Point 1

While you are reading through these examples of development projects you should consider how each of them illustrates the idea of 'sustainable development'.

Netrakona model farm

This farm has been set up with ActionAid money and advice from local farmers and researchers. The aim is to pass on new ideas and to improve farming and health. In particular they encourage people to keep cattle to provide milk for protein. They demonstrate the best ways of looking after cattle to encourage maximum yields.

The model farm also shows how vegetables can be grown, encouraging the use of new varieties such as 'red spinach' which is particularly rich in iron. This helps to tackle the problem of anaemia, which is very common in this area, especially amongst women. Anaemia is debilitating; people who suffer from it are gradually weakened, work less efficiently and become ill more easily. If the anaemia can be tackled simply and cheaply the whole quality of life of the people improves.

Cyclone warning and protection

Bangladesh has good facilities for spotting approaching cyclones and predicting where they will strike. Unfortunately they do not have good communication networks to pass the warnings on to all villages.

ActionAid has set up a series of monitoring posts on Bola Island to listen to radio broadcasts and collect warnings. When the monitors hear warnings they raise red flags outside. The flags have the following meanings:

- 1 flag – don't worry yet, but keep a good lookout

- 2 flags – get ready, tie down the house, bring the boat in, bury supplies of food, make sure that your children are near the house and not playing out of view

- 3 flags – take your cattle to the 'killa' (an earth mound with a dish-shaped top, where cattle can shelter out of the wind and above flood level), take supplies of fresh water and food and get your whole family into the storm shelter.

The government has built some concrete storm shelters around the coast. It has not been able to build enough. ActionAid has financed the building of some shelters on Bola Island. They also use these as schoolrooms. This is partly so that the investment will not be wasted. It is also a way of making people familiar with the shelters, which are very different from the buildings that they are used to.

The role of trans-national corporations (TNCs) in international development

A trans-national corporation is a firm which has branches in at least two countries. They invest money in different countries, outside their home country, for a variety of reasons.

Japanese-based TNCs invested in many countries in the late twentieth century, although recently Japan's economy has not been as strong so this investment has been reduced a little.

ocus Point 2

'Give a man a fish and you feed him for a day; teach him to fish and you feed him for a lifetime.'

'Teach a man and you teach a man; teach a woman and you teach a community.'

What do these two slogans mean?

How are they relevant to ActionAid's work in Bangladesh?

Japanese investment in the Pacific Rim countries

Many Japanese firms invested in LEDCs around the Pacific Rim. They did this because:

- some countries had raw materials that Japanese industry needed, so Japanese firms extracted the materials, e.g. iron ore from Australia, tropical hard woods from Indonesia
- LEDCs have lower wage rates than Japan, so firms assemble their products in LEDCs to cut costs, e.g. Sony have assembly plants in Taiwan and the Philippines
- countries such as South Korea have low tax zones for foreign firms, again allowing the TNC to cut costs
- labour and environment laws are often less strict than in Japan, which again means lower costs.

The TNCs' main aim is to increase company profits. At the same time they have brought advantages and disadvantages to the LEDCs.

Advantages to LEDCs	Disadvantages to LEDCs
Wage rates are higher than those paid by local firms	Work conditions are often poor TNCs may close down their factories – no long-term commitment to the country
Government earns taxes from TNC	Area may be polluted
Some employees receive training	The most skilled jobs often go to outsiders
Resources are developed without the LEDC having to find the capital	The resources might be completely worked out by the TNC
TNC may help to develop infrastructure of roads, ports, etc.	TNCs are not always interested in sustainable development

Japanese investment in the EU

Japanese TNCs have also invested in the EU. Examples are the car plants built by Nissan in Sunderland and by Toyota at Burnaston. These have brought advantages to both the TNC and the UK.

Advantages to the TNC	Advantages to the UK and the region
The company does not need to pay EU tariffs on cars it sells in Europe	The factories bring jobs to areas of high unemployment (which is why government grants are available)
Transport costs are lower than they would be on cars exported from Japan	The Japanese brought new, efficient working methods to the UK industry
Labour costs are cheaper in the UK than in Japan	The government earns tax revenue from company and from the workers
Regional aid is available from the EU and/or the UK to help with capital costs	Other companies are attracted to set up component factories in the area (the multiplier effect)

17 Global warming: its causes and consequences

For this topic you should study:
- factors causing the greenhouse effect:
  - burning fossil fuels
  - destruction of the rainforest
- the consequences of global warming:
  - the rise in sea level
  - the increase in extreme weather events
- attempts to reduce global warming and to manage its consequences.

The greenhouse effect and global warming

This is a subject that is surrounded with controversy. Since the 1960s some scientists have said that global warming is happening, and some have said that it is not. Those who think it is have not all agreed about the speed of change. Some have said it is due to human factors; others believe it is mainly natural.

There have also been disagreements about whether anything can be done to stop or reduce the warming.

The graph shows the changes in global temperatures. It is quite clear now that there have been two periods of very rapid warming, from 1910 to 1940 and again from 1975 to the present.

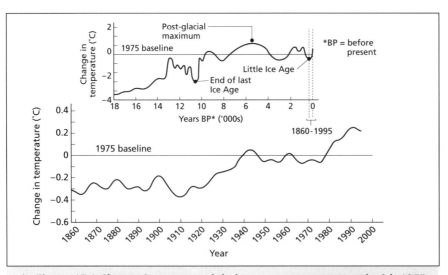

▲ *Figure 17.1 Change in average global temperature compared with 1975 figure*

Hints and Tips!

Warning! Be very careful what you say about global warming. Do not state anything too strongly. You cannot prove or disprove any of the theories, but you can present evidence, and *suggest what might be happening.*

What would be the impact of global warming?

Obviously temperatures would increase, but not evenly all over the globe. The icecaps would melt faster, although some people think that higher temperatures would cause greater evaporation, leading to increased snowfall, so the ice sheets might not actually shrink in size.

Even if the icecaps do not melt, sea level could rise by 1–2 metres over the next 50 years. This could be caused by expansion of the water, due to its increased temperature. This would lead to flooding of many coastal areas. Some island states might disappear altogether. Even more worrying is the threat to many of the world's great food-growing areas on low-lying river floodplains, such as the Ganges delta in Bangladesh. Many great port cities are also found on coasts.

The movement of the wind and pressure belts would lead to a change in the distribution of rainfall over the continents. This could lead to massive changes in agricultural production.

There would certainly be an increase in violent, unstable weather conditions. It is thought that the frequency and strength of tropical storms is already increasing. Floods and droughts may be happening more often too.

If global warming is happening, what is its cause?

The 'greenhouse effect' is a natural process. Some gases, particularly carbon dioxide, but also methane, water vapour and nitrous oxide, allow the sun's rays to pass through the atmosphere and warm the Earth. Then they trap some of the heat and stop it being re-radiated. Without this process the Earth would be too cold for life as we know it.

However, since the Industrial Revolution, people have been burning fossil fuels in ever increasing quantities, and this releases carbon dioxide into the atmosphere. This is probably adding to the natural greenhouse effect.

Destruction of the rainforest and global warming

The trees in the rainforest contain large amounts of carbon. During the process of photosynthesis they take carbon dioxide from the environment and use it to help make new plant material. When areas of rainforest are burnt the carbon in the plant material is released into the atmosphere. This process is described in more detail in chapter 12 on page 99. Check it again now.

Reducing global warming and managing its consequences

This topic was described in chapter 3 on pages 37–38.

Note Some people suggest that global warming might make temperatures in the UK *fall*. This could happen if melting of the Arctic icecap causes changes to the pattern of ocean currents, which could divert the warm North Atlantic Drift away from the British Isles.

ocus Point 1

Re-read this section and pick out five changes that could happen as a result of global warming.

Hints and Tips!

Make sure you understand that the greenhouse effect is a natural process that has been *increased* by human actions.

Short-answer questions, answers and advice on the exam questions

Short answer questions

Both the Foundation and Higher tiers for both Paper 1 and Paper 2 will contain some 'short answer questions' as well as longer, structured questions. At the time of writing this book it is not clear just what form these short questions will take. The questions below suggest some of the ways that these short questions *might* be set.

All these questions refer to the sketch below.

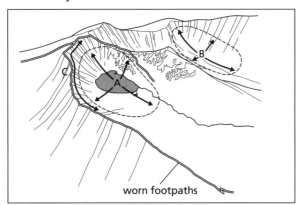

worn footpaths

Study the sketch provided, Figure 1.

1   There are many features that show that this
    area has been glaciated.
    Name the features at A, B and C. Choose your
    answers from the list given below the box.

A	
B	
C	

    corrie   V-shaped valley   arête
    glacial trough   interlocking spur   (3)

2   Label a pyramid peak on the sketch.   (1)

3   During the ice age this area was eroded by
    glaciers. Which **two** of the following are
    common glaciation processes?
    (Underline your **two** choices.)

    hydraulic action   plucking   saltation
    moraine   abrasion   solution   (2)

4   (i) Complete the following sentence by
    writing a word or short phrase in the space.

    The main type of farming in this area is
    _____ farming, which is a
    type of pastoral farming.   (1)

(ii) The soils in this area were affected by
glaciation. Give one way in which glaciation
made the soils in this area unsuitable for
arable farming.

_____ (1)

5   The area shown is
    part of the Lake
    District. Which of
    these figures is most
    likely to show the
    average annual
    rainfall in this area?
    (Tick the correct
    box.)

20 inches	
200 mm	
200 inches	
2000 mm	
20 000 mm	

(1)

6   Give **one** piece of evidence from the sketch
    which shows that this area is popular with
    tourists. _____ (1)

7   This area is part of a National Park. Which of
    the statements below is/are correct?
    (Tick your chosen statement(s).)

The Park authorities own all the land in a National Park.	
Tourists have a right to walk wherever they want in a National Park.	
The Park authorities have a duty to conserve the landscape in a National Park.	
Outsiders are not allowed to buy holiday homes in National Parks.	
The Park authorities have a duty to encourage people to use National Parks for leisure activities.	

(2)

8   Name **two** outdoor activities that the area
    shown in this sketch is very well suited for.

_____   _____ (2)

Answers to short-answer questions

1   A = corrie   B = glacial trough   C = arête

2   1cm down and 3.5cm in from the right.

3   plucking   abrasion

4   (i) sheep, or hill sheep

(ii) Glaciers scraped the soil off much of the higher land.

5   2000mm

6   The footpaths have been worn away and are very wide.

7   The Park authorities have a duty to conserve the landscape in a National Park.

The Park authorities have a duty to encourage people to use National Parks for leisure activities.

8   walking   rock climbing   mountain biking   orienteering   bird watching

The activities above are obviously correct. Others might go on here, but are much less obviously correct. Do answer sensibly.
(**Not** boating or sailing – the corrie lake is too remote.)

1 River basins and their management (page 15)

(a) The three parts of (a) are all linked, but each part needs different skills. You must name a real example in (i) but make sure you choose an example that you can describe in enough detail to gain 3 marks in (ii). When you describe the feature try to show 'a sense of place'. Describe a real place, not a diagram. If possible, describe somewhere you have been and studied in the field. If that is not possible, describe an example that you have seen in photos or on videos.

In (iii) you need to be more theoretical. The 'command' part of (iii) tells you to 'use one or more diagrams'. You can also include extended writing, or you can put your explanations as labels on the diagram. It is very important that you know how to draw these diagrams quickly but accurately. The best way to make sure you can do this is to get plenty of practice. Select some of the diagrams and maps from this book and draw them as often as you can. Each time you should get better, quicker and more detailed. Learning the diagram should help you to learn a set of ideas and to visualise how different processes and/or places are linked together.

(b) (i) The key points here are
   • the basin structure of the rocks
   • the presence of a permeable layer of rock between two impermeable layers
   • rainfall from the Chilterns and South Downs percolating through the chalk
   • wells being drilled down to the water table.

Again, learning the diagram should help you to understand and learn all these points.

(ii) The Thames; purified, recycled water.

(c) There are many possible examples. It is probably best for you to learn details of your own local example.

2 Farming, food and the environment (page 24)

(a) (i) Note that **all** you are asked for here is a diagram. You are not asked for any extended writing, but you need to add clear written labels to your diagram. Drawing diagrams is an important skill that you should practise carefully. Check the diagram on page 20 of this book. Make sure that you have learnt it precisely.

(ii) You could answer this questions with a diagram or extended writing. In a geography exam you will always get credit for using relevant technical terms. Here, the obvious term to use is 'rain shadow'. If you have not used that term in your answer, make sure that you know it. Use it next time!

(b) Before you can explain you probably need to give a brief description of the relief of the two areas. The obvious point to make here is that the steep slopes in the Lake District are not suitable for the machines used by arable farmers, but the gentle slopes of East Anglia are suitable. That alone will not get the full 5 marks. You need to think about this **geographically**.

Steep slopes often have thin soils, because rainwater washes the soil down (erosion). Thicker soils can develop on gentle slopes. If you can think through points like this and make connections between different aspects of the physical and human geography of an area, you will gain high marks.

(c) This question contains two 'command words': **describe** and **explain**.

Describe tells you to say *what* is there. To do this you need carefully learnt knowledge about a real place.

Explain tells you to say *why* it is there. Here you need to develop ideas and show how things are linked together. In this part of your answer you need to show connections. Use phrases like:
'If the farmer does this he will benefit because ...'
'Doing this is good for the soil because ...'
'Growing these crops reduces the costs and increases profits because ...'

3 Tourism in a glacial environment: the Lake District National Park (page 33)

(a) To conserve unspoilt countryside, and to encourage access. Both parts for 1 mark. These are basic ideas that **must** be learnt.

(b) (i) Before you choose the feature, make sure you **read the whole question**. There is only 1 mark for choosing the feature, but 7 marks for what you write about it!

(ii) **Describe** just means 'say what it looks like'. For 2 marks you need some detail, but do not explain *why* it is like that.

(iii) Here explanation *is* needed. Questions about glacial processes mean abrasion and plucking. Learn about them!

When the question says 'You may use a diagram', it is always best to draw one. Diagrams summarise information in a very clear way. Learn to draw diagrams as part of your revision.

(c) (i) A simple idea needs a simple, clear definition. Learn it, with examples.

(iii) The question gives you two ideas: 'honeypot sites' and 'the areas around them'. Write about each. With 4 marks available you are expected to elaborate.

e.g. 'Areas around honeypot sites like Tarn Hows often suffer traffic congestion on the narrow roads. This can delay tourists, but it also causes problems for farmers trying to make a living in the area.'

4 Electricity generation for the future (page 40)

(a) Check your answers with the maps on page 35 and page 39.

(b) If you chose the Trent valley you could say:

'This area is close to the Notts coalfield and close to the River Trent for water supply.' This would probably gain you 2 marks. To gain the full 4 marks you could write:

'This area is close to the Notts coalfield so the cost of transporting bulky fuel to the power stations is reduced. Power stations are built along the River Trent so they have plenty of water for cooling the steam so that it can be recycled.' In other words, **develop** and **elaborate** your points.

(c) Refer to some of the following: high rainfall, low evaporation, large catchment area, steep slopes, narrow valleys for dams, impermeable rocks, cheap land for reservoirs, etc. Once again, try to develop and elaborate the simple ideas listed.

(d) When nuclear stations were first being developed they were built in remote areas (e.g. Calder Hall, Dounreay) for safety reasons. Later stations (e.g. Hartlepool, Dungeness) were built closer to cities because it was cheaper to transport the electricity over short distances.

(e) Coal and gas are non-renewable resources; wind and solar power are renewable. Burning fossil fuels helps to cause global warming. Burning coal helps to cause acid rain, etc.

5 The changing locations of manufacturing industry (page 47)

(a) (i) Estuaries provide sheltered ports for importing raw materials and exporting finished goods. Rivers provide a source of fresh water for industrial processes and cleaning.

(ii) Tees, Thames, Southampton Water, Avon, Mersey. (These are the main ones.)

(b) Check your answers with page 43 in this book, or your own notes. You will need knowledge like this if you are aiming for a high grade. The only way to make sure of this knowledge is by hard learning.

(c) The key idea here is that the waste materials of one chemical plant often become the raw materials for another. Explain and illustrate that idea by referring to named examples of plants, the raw materials that each uses, and the finished products that are manufactured there.

(d) Refer to some of the following:
- Good transport links, especially motorways and airports.
- The knowledge base of the area in universities and research establishments.
- The close links between firms in the high-tech sector.
- The large, rich market nearby – London, the South East, Midlands, Europe.
- The attractive environment encourages skilled workers to move into the area.

Try to give the name of a place, an area or a firm to illustrate each point that you make.

6 Understanding the modern urban environment (page 56)

Note how this question is laid out. At the start of (a) you are told to name a town. Then there is a series of questions labelled (i) to (iv). The town that you name has to be used to illustrate your answers to **all** parts of (a). Before you rush into your answer, read the whole of question (a). This will help you choose your town or city wisely. Try to be sure that you can answer all four sections using information about the town you choose. You should be very careful that your town can be used for part (iv) – because that section has most marks!

Then, at the start of (b), there is another instruction. The area that you have to name here must be used for all parts of (b). However, the town that you named in (a) does not have to be used here. The way the question is laid out means that the first instruction 'Name an industrial town or city ...' only applies to (a).

(a) (ii) Note that there are 2 marks available for this answer, but you are only asked for one reason. This quite clearly means that you must develop or elaborate your answer. A single phrase is not enough.

e.g. 'It had to be on a coalfield for power.' This would only get 1 mark because it only has one simple idea.

'It had to be on a coalfield because it needed a source of power, and coal was so bulky that it would have been too expensive to transport it a long distance.' This would easily gain the second mark because the reason is explained in some detail.

(iii) Again you need to elaborate your answer for full marks.

e.g. 'The houses were packed close together as near as possible to the docks.' One idea gets 1 mark.

'The houses were built in the area called Byker. They were packed close together as near as possible to the docks.' Here a good, named example is given, and this precision gains the extra mark.

(iv) There are two parts to this question, and 4 marks. Write clearly elaborated and developed points to describe both the houses and the street pattern.

e.g. 'The workers' houses in Salford were brick-built terraced houses and most of them had two rooms downstairs and two bedrooms. Many of them did not have inside toilets but just a privy at the bottom of the yard. The streets were usually laid out in a rectangular pattern with people's front doors opening straight onto the pavement.'

(b) Your answer will depend on the area that you have chosen. However, you must try to develop your points in detail. There are 4 marks for each section, so the examiner will expect extended writing and logical development of ideas. Precise references to the chosen area are also needed.

(c) e.g. 'London is a perfect example of a city with commuter villages and towns. They developed because many people worked in the city but could afford to live out in the countryside and then travel to work by car, train or underground. Lilley near Luton is a commuter village with lovely big houses in an unpolluted environment.'

(page 60)

(a) Exams may include 'story'-type questions like this. Do not be distracted. This is still a geography exam, and you will only get marks for knowledge and understanding of geography. What is this testing?

Concentrate on the idea that private cars offer much greater flexibility than public transport does. Cars can go to more places, and are usually quicker than buses or trains, especially over short distances.

(b) This question deals with the downside of car transport. In (i) you should write about the loss of the countryside and/or the damage done to areas in towns and cities. Give an example of an area that has been affected, if you can. In (ii) you could write about accidents, atmospheric pollution, or exhaustion of oil resources. Be as precise as possible. 'Cars cause pollution' will not gain many marks. 'Cars cause air pollution by releasing nitrous oxides which cause acid rain' will gain far more credit.

(c) To answer this question needs detailed local knowledge. Your answer could be written at different scales, e.g. describe a small-scale scheme to pedestrianise a street in a small town; or write about a city-wide plan such as construction of Sheffield's Supertram system.

Try to keep your answer in two separate sections. Describe the scheme first: where it is located and what is being done. Then give a clear explanation of the theory behind the scheme. You are not asked to comment on the success of the scheme, but there is no harm in giving your views if they are explained briefly and are supported by evidence.

8 Farming in southern Italy (page 67)

(a) (i) You must learn where to mark this boundary on the map. Check on page 63.

(ii) The 'easy catchphrase' is the best way to remember this:
- Hot dry summers (with easterly winds)
- Warm wet winters (with westerly winds).

The best candidates for the exam will learn statistics to illustrate their answers. Are you aiming to get a good mark? Have you learnt the statistics?

(iii) There is 1 mark for describing the relief. The other marks are for explaining how the relief affects soil, suitability of the land for machinery, etc.

(iv) They mainly produce food for the family who farm the land. Their main aim is not to produce cash crops for the market.

(v) The main markets are in northern Italy and further north in the EU (1 mark). Southern Italy is distant from this market and road links are still poor (2nd mark).

(b) (i) The office for the development of the southern region of Italy.

(ii) You have to choose any of the following policies listed under these headings on page 66:

Farming improvements
- Took land from the big absentee landlords and broke it up into small plots.
- Small farmers were given cheap loans to invest in farm improvements.
- Agricultural colleges were set up to introduce new methods to the area.
- Reforestation schemes and river control schemes were introduced.

Infrastructure
- Roads to link rural areas to the towns, and to link the South to the North.
- Drainage and sewerage systems, to improve health.
- Water supply, for domestic use and to improve irrigation.
- Electricity supply.

Industrial development, health care, etc.
- Increased employment opportunities.
- Raised living standards.
- Increased local market for agricultural produce.

(iii) The EU policy to develop the poor agricultural areas in southern Europe.

(iv) Its policies include:

Farming
- Improve olive and vine growing.
- Improve animal care, especially through better veterinary care.
- Improve market organisations.

Creating off-farm jobs
- Craft activities.
- Small-scale industries.
- Small hotels, campsites, etc.

Other activities
- Improve fishing by modernising ports and buying new boats.
- Extend forestry and reduce soil erosion.
- Education and training.

(c) Describe some of the achievements and some of the problems that remain. You must also attempt to summarise whether the policies have been successful or not. The Mezzogiorno still has problems, but would they be even worse without the Cassa and the IMP?

9 Tourism in Mediterranean Spain (page 71)

(a) (i) See the answer to question (a)(ii) in Chapter 8. You should try to use statistics in your answer. You will not gain full marks unless you do.

(ii) Natural attractions include coastal scenery and scenery inland. This includes the rocks and the vegetation. Try to give some detail on this. Many examiners are impressed by 'traditional geography' of rocks and vegetation. Also describe the sea and the beaches. Many areas are very safe, with an absence of strong currents and tides.

(b) Learn the location of the costas and one or two resorts on each. If you have visited any Spanish resorts you might find it easy to learn details about them, rather than places you have just read about.

(c) (i) Many people will answer 'well-paid jobs'. This may gain a mark, but you would be far better answering 'There is a variety of jobs, including well-paid work for trained people, such as hotel managers, but unskilled people can get jobs like chambermaids, and these are better-paid than the traditional farming and fishing jobs.'

(ii) Again many people will give a simple answer by referring to 'pollution'. The topic can easily be developed to discuss the noise pollution brought by aeroplanes or by people leaving clubs in the early hours of the morning. You could also refer to loss of the natural landscape, which may destroy the attractions of the resorts.

(d) This is a 2 mark answer, so it needs some development. You could refer to growth of holidays in inland Spain, investment in new facilities, advertising in new markets in eastern Europe, etc. Whichever theme you choose needs to be illustrated with specific examples.

10 Development of the European urban core (pages 89-90)

The first part of this question asks you to apply your knowledge and understanding of the European core region. The question presents you with details about a different part of the core and asks you to analyse that data.

Read the introduction to the question carefully. It shows that the question is going to be about planning and the planners' response to an issue in the conurbation. Then the second paragraph of the introduction refers to the position of Lille within the core of Europe. Then look at part (a).

(a) The map in Figure 10.14 emphasises that position. You should be able to work out that Lille is right on the border between France and Belgium with close links to the Netherlands, Luxemburg, Germany and to the UK across the Channel. It also has an excellent road and rail network.

This should lead to you answering that these excellent links should allow Lille to develop a variety of new services and industries serving large parts of the core region. As this region is the main growth area of the EU it should provide a very big and prosperous market. Perhaps you could make reference to the part of the core that you have studied, and show how access to that area might help Lille's development.

(b) (i) Now you look at the second map, Figure 10.15. This shows metro lines and tram lines linking together many of the suburbs and outlying towns of the conurbation. It also shows the links between these systems of public transport and the road network. Use your knowledge and understanding of other urban areas (in the UK as well as the European core) to draw some conclusions about Lille's development.

(ii) Figure 10.16 shows some of Lille's growth poles. The key gives details of the types of industries and services they are designed to attract. You only need to gain two marks. Refer to two of the poles, name the type of

development that is planned in each area, and then explain why Lille is good for that. For example:

Lomme is built near to good transport links to the UK, so it will be attractive to UK firms wanting to trade in France.

La Haute Borne is designed for high-tech industry, which needs attractive sites on the rural urban fringe.

(iii) Develop the ideas from (ii) in this part of the answer. For example:

Euralille is in the centre of the conurbation. It is close to the transport node, so it will be accessible to business people from all over the continent who might travel by high speed train. The centre of the city will have a dynamic image. People who work here will be able to make easy contacts with banks and other financial services and this will help them grow and develop new contacts.

(c) Finally, you have a 9 mark question (although 6 marks would probably be the maximum on a Foundation Paper.) This tests your knowledge of your chosen urban core region. The question is asked in two parts. It is best to write two quite separate sections for an answer like this. You will not get full marks unless you do both parts fully, and dividing the answer up makes sure that you do both parts well.
Note that there are two different command words – 'describe' and 'explain'. The first asks for facts and the second asks for reasoning. Make sure that you practice both types of writing.
A map might well help your answer. However, most people cannot just make a map up in their exam. For a fairly predictable question like this it is probably worth learning a map during your revision.

11 The links between eastern England and the EU (page 94)

(a) (i) Check your answer with the map on page 92.

(ii) This means its links with other parts of the UK, where industry and population are growing, and also means links across the Channel with Europe. You should refer to the growth of trade with the EU.

(iii) Try to make reference to named roads.

(iv) Give details of ro-ro ferries, container-handling facilities and other bulk-handling systems. Ports have become more capital intensive and have cut labour.

(b) (i) Dover

(ii) The Tunnel has damaged the cross-Channel ferry trade. However, you should try to suggest how the ferry companies might fight back (amalgamations, new and better ferries, etc.).

12　Amazonia: development in the rainforest environment (page 101)

(a) (i) The key point that you must make is that there is very little seasonal change. Average monthly temperatures are high at all times. You should quote figures, especially if you are entered for the Higher paper. The average monthly temperature is about 27°C, with a range of only 2–3 degrees.

(Note that in a real exam you would probably be given a graph that showed temperature in a particular place. You would be asked to interpret the graph.)

(ii) The sun's rays are concentrated close to the Equator at all seasons. It would be a good idea to learn to draw a diagram showing this, so that you can draw it in the exam. A good diagram earns good marks with less effort than writing a full explanation.

(b) Here the question says 'You may use a diagram ...'. The examiner really means 'You **should** use a diagram if you can because it is a good way of showing geographical information'. The 4 marks are allocated for:
• heating the ground
• air on the ground is heated and rises
• as air rises it cools
• causing condensation, clouds and rainfall.

(c) (i) Each definition needs a clear sentence – or a diagram. These terms should be learnt. There is 1 mark for each definition.

(ii) Whichever feature you choose, your first 2 marks will come from these points:
• heat and moisture are always available, so plants grow quickly
• plants struggle upwards, competing for sunlight
• soils are thin, because nutrients are taken up quickly by growing plants.

The third mark will come for linking the rapid growth of plants to the feature you have chosen.

(d) You should explain that these problems affect people at different scales.

Exposed soil causes problems for local people when it is eroded, but people downstream can be affected by deposition blocking the river, causing floods.

Reduced evapotranspiration can affect people deeper in the rainforest, because it reduces the amount of water in the air, which leads to reduced rainfall.

Forest fires can get out of control and damage the local area. Smoke can blow over nearby regions, causing pollution and breathing problems. Carbon dioxide adds to the greenhouse effect, so it may affect the global climate.

To gain a high-level mark you must look at some of the problems outside the local area.

(e) (i) Obviously eco-tourism is a very specialised type of holiday. It involves adventure, learning and seeing incredible sights, very different from anything in the UK or in 'standard' holiday resorts. Explain this.

(ii) Local people will benefit from work and income, obviously. However, a high-level answer needs to show more detailed understanding that this. Eco-tourism involves protecting environments and cultures from other forms of development. So explain how the local people might benefit from the conservation or sustainable development aspects of eco-tourism.

13　The Ganges delta: dense population in a high-risk environment (page 110)

(a) (i) Here is a simple 1 mark answer: 'Sediment is deposited by a river.'

Here is an elaborated 2 mark answer: 'The river current slows down when it reaches the sea. It loses energy and drops sediment, building a delta in the shallow sea.'

(ii) A stream that carries some of the water from a river across a delta. (1 mark)

(iii) There are two separate points needed here. 'It is formed from fine sediment.' (1 mark) 'The sediment is renewed every year by floods.' (1 mark)

(b) (i) For a 7 mark answer you ought to plan to write about 12–15 lines.
• For the nature of cyclones you should refer to the wind and heavy rain, and to the waves that are whipped up. Try to give some detail for each point.
• Refer to the low, flat land and the absence of natural barriers to the wind or waves. You may also refer to the possibility of relief rainfall, which adds river water to the floods from the sea.

- The low level of development means that barriers to stop flooding are not well developed. The area does not have good resources to cope after the cyclone, leading to short-term and long-term problems. For example: in the short term people are trapped and cannot be rescued; in the longer term disease spreads because of lack of clean water.

(ii) The answer will depend on the scheme chosen. Give precise facts and write in enough detail to gain all 3 marks available.

(page 114)

(a) (i) This needs a two-part answer. Each part needs elaboration to gain full marks, e.g.
- There is a high death rate, especially amongst children, so people need many babies to be sure that one or two survive.
- There is no social security, so families need a son to support them in old age.

(ii) In some ways the answer to this is the reverse of the answer above. It needs to be explained clearly and concisely.
- If there is a high death rate, people have many babies to make sure that at least one survives. The birth rate will only fall when people are more certain their babies will survive to become adults.

(b) (i)

Stage	1	2	3	4
Death rate	high	starts to fall	still falling	low
Birth rate	high	high	starts to fall	low
Total population	low	rising at an increasing rate	still rising, but at a slower rate	high, but now stable

1 mark each time birth rate and death rate are both correct in a stage.   (4 x 1)

Award 1 mark for each correct total.   (4 x 1)

(ii) Death rate starts to fall because of new medical discoveries.   (2 x 1)

(iii) Birth rates fall because couples see benefits of limiting family size.   (2 x 1)

In (ii) and (iii) the first mark is for a simple correct statement. The second mark is for elaboration or explanation.

14 Japan: urbanisation and industrialisation in a resource-poor environment (page 121)

(a) (i) Choose any two from: coal, oil, natural gas, nuclear.

(ii) Choose any two from geothermal, HEP, wave, wind.

(iii) The answer will depend on the source of energy chosen. To get full marks, give clear, detailed elaboration. Describe the conditions needed for the form of energy then show how Japan meets the requirements of that form of energy.

(b) (i) The answers are given on the map on page 118. Learn all four major industrial regions. Yes, of course the names are difficult to learn because they are in a foreign language, but you must try.

(ii) Two key ideas are:
- most raw materials are imported
- almost all of the flat land suitable for urban settlement is close to the coast.

Each key idea should be elaborated to gain full marks.

(iii) Refer to investment in research and development of new products.

15 Population growth and urbanisation (page 128)

1 mark for naming a city.
Pushes Shortage of land. High birth rate. Not enough food. Little chance of education or advancement in rural areas, etc.

Pulls Possibility of jobs in city. 'Bright lights' of city. More chance of education in city, etc.

Do try not to give direct opposites on your 'pushes' and 'pulls', e.g. 'jobs', 'no jobs' will not get 2 separate marks.

Index

aid 129–32
alternative energy 38–40, 116
Amazonia 95–101
arable farming 17
arétes 28

Bangladesh
 aid 130–2
 population 108–13

Calcutta 124–7
capital intensive farming 17
Cassa per il Mezzogiorno 66–7
central business district (CBD) 49, 57–8
chemical industries 42–4
climate
 Mediterranean Spain 68
coal 34, 36, 77–9, 115
commercial farming 17
conurbations 50–1, 86–7
corries 28
cyclones 103–5

deforestation 98–9, 105
demographic transition model 111–13
Disneyland 84–5
Dover 91–3
drainage basins
 definition 9
 landforms 9–12
 movement of water 7–9
 water management 13–15

East Anglia 19, 22–3
eco-tourism 100–1
electricity generation 34–40
environmental issues
 electricity generation 36–8
 farming 20–1, 24, 98–100
 Japan 120–1
 pollution 14, 22, 52
 Ruhr conurbation 79–81
erosion 9, 27
European Union (EU) 21, 61–95, 133
Europort 73, 75
extensive farming 17

farming
 Amazonia 98
 chemical inputs 22
 classification 16–17
 development, India 108–10
 diversification 21–2
 environmental issues 20–1, 24
 Lake District 18
 Southern Italy 63–7
 systems 16–17
flood control 14, 76, 106–7
flooding 75–6, 103–7
freeze-thaw weathering 27

Ganges delta 102–10
gas 34, 36–7
glaciation 27–9
global warming 37–8, 134–5
Green Revolution, India 108–9
greenfield sites 50
greenhouse effect see global warming

heavy industry 77–9
HEP 35–6
high-rise housing 53
high-technology industries 45–6, 118–20
'honeypot' management 30–1
housing patterns 54
hydrological cycle 7

India
 Green Revolution 108–9
 population 110–14
industrial towns 50–1
industry
 chemical 42–4, 73–4
 heavy 77–82
 hi-tech 45–6, 118–20
 Japan 116–21
 manufacturing 41–7, 116–20
 Milan/Turin/Genoa 86–9
 retail 57–8
 Ruhr conurbation 77–82
inner city decline 52–5
intensive farming 17, 20–1
intermediate technology 109–10
investment, Japanese 133

labour intensive farming 17
Lake District National Park 25–33
leisure and tourism 25–33
low-rise/high-density housing 53

M4 corridor 45–6
manufacturing industry 41–7, 116–20
MEDCs (more economically developing countries) 37, 112–13
Mediterranean Spain, tourism 68–71
Merseyside, chemical industry 42–4
Middlesbrough, population movement 55
monsoons 103

National Parks 25–33
nuclear power 35–6

out-of-town shopping centres 57–8

Paris 83–5
pastoral farming 17
petrochemical industries 73–4
pollution 14, 22, 52
 see also environmental issues

population
 control 113–14
 India and Bangladesh 110–14
 Japan 117
 movement 55, 65
 pyramids 122–3
 structures 122
 urban areas 55–6
ports 91–3
 Rotterdam/Europort 72–6
push and pull factors 53, 66, 123

rainfall 7, 8, 20, 64, 68, 99, 103
renewable energy 36
retail industry 57–8
ribbon development 50
ribbon lakes 28
rice 107
river systems 7–15
Rotterdam/Europort 72–6
Ruhr industrial conurbation 77–82

second homes 31
shanty towns 125–7
slum clearance 52
solar power 40
southern Italy, farming 63–7
Spain, Mediterranean 68–71
subsistence farming 17, 107

Teesside, chemical industry 42–4
thermal power stations 34–5
tourism
 see also leisure and tourism
 Mediterranean Spain 68–71
Trans-national corporations 132
transport
 Channel Tunnel 93–4
 environmental issues 59
 Ferries 93
 rail 74
 roads 59–60, 74
 waterways 74
tropical rainforests 95–101

U-shaped valleys 28–9
United Kingdom 7–60
urban growth 84, 124–8

water management 13–15
water sources 13–14
waterways 74
wind power 39–40